THE TESTAMENT OF THE LORD

ST VLADIMIR'S SEMINARY PRESS
Popular Patristics Series
Number 58

The Popular Patristics Series published by St Vladimir's Seminary Press provides readable and accurate translations of a wide range of early Christian literature to a wide audience—students of Christian history to lay Christians reading for spiritual benefit. Recognized scholars in their fields provide short but comprehensive and clear introductions to the material. The texts include classics of Christian literature, thematic volumes, collections of homilies, letters on spiritual counsel, and poetical works from a variety of geographical contexts and historical backgrounds. The mission of the series is to mine the riches of the early Church and to make these treasures available to all.

The Testament of the Lord

AN ENGLISH VERSION

With an Introduction and Notes by

ALISTAIR C. STEWART

ST VLADIMIR'S SEMINARY PRESS
YONKERS, NEW YORK
2018

Library of Congress Cataloging-in-Publication Data

Names: Stewart, Alistair C. (Alistair Charles), 1960- author of introduction, translator.
Title: The Testament of the Lord : an English version / translated, with an introduction and notes, by Alistair C. Stewart.
Other titles: Testamentum domini. English.
Description: Yonkers, NY : St Vladimir's Seminary Press, 2018. | Series: Popular Patristics Series ; number 58 | Includes bibliographical references.
Identifiers: LCCN 2017058344 (print) | LCCN 2018013707 (ebook) | ISBN 9780881416121 | ISBN 9780881416114 (perm. paper)
Subjects: LCSH: Testamentum domini—Criticism, Textual. | Church orders, Ancient. | Church discipline.
Classification: LCC BS2960.T5 (ebook) | LCC BS2960.T5 A3 2018 (print) | DDC 270.2—dc23
LC record available at https://lccn.loc.gov/2017058344

575 Scarsdale Road, Yonkers, NY 10707
1-800-204-2665
www.svspress.com

ISBN 978-0-88141-611-4 (paper)
ISBN 978-0-88141-612-1 (electronic)
ISSN 1555-5755

PRINTED IN THE UNITED STATES OF AMERICA

Floreat Domus Codringtoniensis

Contents

Preface

The work presented here was first suggested to me by Fr John Behr in 1999, but not started until 2007, after he had reminded me of his request. For a number of years, however, it was abandoned as other projects took precedence, and I despaired of my own ability to complete it. Nonetheless, an invitation from Codrington College to lecture on apocalyptic in the patristic period led to the publication of an article on the apocalyptic section of the *Testament*. Work restarted in earnest in 2015, at Fr John's suggestion that I take it up again. Not for the first time I have cause to thank Fr John and all at St Vladimir's Seminary Press for their confidence in me and for their patience.

In essence this is a translation of the Syriac text published by Rahmani in 1899, though on occasion I have understood this text differently from previous translators. Moreover, on occasion I have ventured a conjecture, and have had an eye to the Ethiopic version, and to the portions of other texts that have been published. As I note in the introduction, this falls short of what is really required, given the complexity of the textual transmission of the work and the extent to which it has been neglected, but if this serves in any way to reignite the interest of specialists, then that is good. The Arabic witnesses in particular need proper investigation.

My primary aim, however, is to make the work better known and readily accessible to a wide readership. Thus although the footnotes may refer to abstruse matters and to recondite secondary literature, the text can be read without reference to them, as can the introduction.

This introduction is intended to show the importance of this neglected work for liturgical history, beyond its value as a witness to *Apostolic Tradition*. Moreover, I hope to have established the (already suspected) fourth-century and Cappadocian provenance of the *Testament*; it is thus a work contemporary with the Cappadocian fathers. A Basilian outlook underlies the *Testament*, which is reason enough, beyond its valuable liturgical information, to read the work.

William Gordon, preaching at the funeral of Christopher Codrington in 1710, noted that Codrington "was a great Admirer of the Fathers, particularly of St. Basil." Sadly, we must record that he followed Basil in accepting the necessity of slavery; however, his bequest for the foundation of a Basilian monastic community in Barbados, whilst never realized, was the basis for the College that I was privileged once to serve, and through which the learning of the fathers is kept alive in the West Indies.

For this we glorify you, we bless you, we give thanks to you, O Lord.

Chalvey, Slough (England)
On the feast of St Ignatius of Antioch, 2017

Introduction

1: The Testament of the Lord

The *Testament of the Lord* is an example of the literature collectively known as the "church orders." The definition of a church order is uncertain and there is scholarly debate even regarding the legitimacy of the term, but it conveniently covers a number of documents that have in common an aim to direct the conduct of Christians and of the church on the basis of an appeal to tradition derived from or mediated through the apostles. This is what the *Testament* does; it describes the building of a church, the mode of appointment for ministers and their duties, and the conduct of daily prayers and of other liturgies, based, it states, on a revelation made by Jesus to his apostles after the resurrection, and transmitted to the church through them. The title, *Testament of the Lord*, refers to the direct attribution of these instructions to Christ.

This particular church order was first published in its entirety in 1899.[1] This was a Syriac translation of a Greek original, and in the Syriac churches formed the first two books of an eight-book collection of church orders known as the Clementine Octateuch.[2] Previously a part of this Syriac text had been published by Lagarde from a single manuscript containing a canonical collection,[3] and thus excerpting from the *Testament*. However, although the turn of

[1]By Ignatius Ephraem II Rahmani, *Testamentum Domini nostri Jesu Christi* (Mainz: Kirchheim, 1899).

[2]This collection of eight books is made up of *Testament of the Lord* (in two books), *Apostolic Church Order*, and book eight of the *Apostolic Constitutions* (divided between four books), to which the *Apostolic Canons* are appended (thus forming an eighth book.)

[3]P. de Lagarde, *Reliquiae iuris ecclesiastici antiquissimae, graece et syriace* (Leipzig: Teubner, 1856), 2–19. The manuscript is now classified as Paris BN Syr. 62.

the twentieth century was a period of intense research in the church order literature, interest tailed off and it was not until 1984 that an Ethiopic translation was published.[4] Further material from the Testament was included in the collection of canons (in Syriac) known as the west Syrian *Synodicon*, published in 1975–76.[5] This, like the manuscript published by Lagarde, shows that the *Testament* continued to be used as a source for canon law, but neither is a complete text. The Arabic versions remain unedited apart from a version of the mystagogy,[6] and a liturgical extract.[7]

In the period immediately following the publication of the *Testament*, the relationship between *Apostolic Tradition* and certain clearly related church order documents—the others, apart from the *Testament*, being the eighth book of the *Apostolic Constitutions* and the *Canons of Hippolytus*—was much debated. The emergence of a consensus[8] that *Apostolic Tradition* was the source of the other documents certainly contributed to the loss of interest in the later church orders, as well as making much of the earlier discussion somewhat redundant. The *Testament* was considered late, derivative, and uninteresting. However, I will suggest that the *Testament* may be seen of value in its own right; conclusions reached concerning its date and

[4]Roger Beylot, *Testamentum Domini éthiopien: Édition et traduction* (Leuven: Peeters, 1984).

[5]Arthur Vööbus, ed., *The Synodicon in the West Syrian Tradition,* 2 vols. in 4 pts., Corpus Scriptorum Christianorum Orientalium 367–378, 375–376 (Leuven: Peeters, 1975/76).

[6]Published by O. Burmeister, "The Coptic and Arabic Versions of the Mystagogia," *Le Muséon* 46 (1933): 203–235, from the Borgian Arabic known to Rahmani.

[7]Gérard Troupeau, "Une version arabe de l'anaphore du *Testamentum Domini,*" in *Christianisme oriental: kérygme et histoire; mélanges offerts au père Michel Hayek*, ed. Charles Chartouni (Paris: Librairie orientaliste Paul Geuthner, 2007), 247–256. Baumstark also published a liturgical fragment from an Arabic manuscript containing the *Testament* ("Eine aegyptische Meß- und Taufliturgie vermutlich des 6. Jahrhunderts," *Oriens Christianus* 1 [1901]: 1–45), but this is not part of the text of the *Testament* itself.

[8]The result of the independent works of E. Schwartz, *Über die pseudapostolischen Kirchenordnungen*, Schriften der wissenschaftlichen Gesellschaft im Strassburg 6 (Strassburg: Trübner, 1910) and R. H. Connolly, *The So-Called Egyptian Church Order and Derived Documents* (Cambridge: Cambridge University Press, 1916).

provenance, which have formed the basis for the consensus and yet were based on an incomplete understanding of the relationship of the *Testament* and the *Apostolic Tradition*, must be abandoned and the question entirely re-examined,[9] and so the intrinsic interest and value of the *Testament*, beyond its use as a source for the reconstruction of *Apostolic Tradition*, will be demonstrated.[10]

The translation presented here is basically a fresh translation of the Syriac text published in 1899, though some effort is made to compare this with readings from the Ethiopic and elsewhere, and a few conjectures are made. However, to avoid overloading the reader, a certain selectivity has been employed in noting variants between the texts. Scholars who recognize that this does not count much as a scientific advance are referred to the section of the introduction below, dealing in more detail with the text and the issue of transmission, and gently reminded that they are not the primary audience. The intended audience for this translation is readers who want some idea of the contents of the *Testament* out of interest in liturgical, historical, or ascetical theology. To them the apology is offered that on occasion the meaning of the *Testament* is so unclear that the translator's sole recourse is to render what is there, even if it seems devoid of meaning, though his main purpose is to produce a readable and accessible translation.

2: The Text of the Testament

As has already been noted, the first publication of any substantial portion of the *Testament* was that of Lagarde, who in 1858 published

[9]As an example of the conclusions reached at the time based on this failure of understanding, we may note J. Wordsworth, "The 'Testament of our Lord.' Part II: Its Connexion with the School of Apollinarius of Laodicea," *Church Quarterly Review* 99 (1900): 1–29, which contends that the *Testament* was an Apollinarian response to the (Arian) *Apostolic Constitutions* 8. Funk similarly believed that the *Testament*, as well as the *Canons of Hippolytus*, were derivations from *Apostolic Constitutions* 8.

[10]The characterization of the *Testament* by J. N. D. Kelly as "a post-Nicene rehash of . . . *Apostolic Tradition*, probably dating from the fifth century" typifies the attitude of much twentieth-century scholarship to this document. *Early Christian Creeds*, 3rd ed. (London: Longman, 1972), 35.

the contents of a Parisian manuscript containing canonical material.[11] Rahmani's edition was based on a single Syriac manuscript at Mosul, though he also had reference to a further Syriac manuscript at Rome,[12] to Lagarde's text, and to a single Arabic manuscript, also at Rome, which he took to be a translation from Coptic.[13]

As has already been noted, the *Testament* is also extant in Ethiopic and Arabic. Although the Arabic is unedited apart from the fragment given by Troupeau,[14] a remarkable study of the manuscripts was undertaken by Coquin, who concludes on the basis of a sampling of readings and examination of mistranslations and misunderstandings by various translators, that there were no less than three recensions of the Greek represented by the extant versions. One is represented by the Borgian Arabic manuscript employed by Rahmani, one by Rahmani's Syriac version (and, he suggests, by the Ethiopic), and one by two distinct Arabic versions, one, he believes, derived directly from the Greek, and one through a Coptic intermediary.[15] The Ethiopic version presents further problems. Although Coquin concludes that it is derived directly from Greek, and represents the same Greek recension that Jacob translated into Syriac, the Ethiopic version's editor, Beylot, tended to prefer readings already supported by Rahmani's Syriac text, which, as Cowley notes in a review, is a procedure that does not help in answering questions regarding "the existence of recensions of the Ethiopic text, its (or their) relationship to the Syriac and Arabic versions, and the possibility of a Greek original."[16]

[11]Paris BN Syr. 62, known at the time as Codex Sangermanensis 38.

[12]Borg. Syr. 148.

[13]Borg. Ar. 22. This manuscript is discussed and described by Anton Baumstark, "Die arabischen Texte der *Diathēkē tou Kuriou*," *Römische Quartalschrift* 14 (1900): 291–300.

[14]Troupeau, "Version arabe."

[15]René-Georges Coquin, "Le Testamentum Domini: problèmes de tradition textuelle," *Parole de l'Orient* 5 (1974): 165–188.

[16]Roger Cowley, review of Beylot in *Journal of Semitic Studies* 31 (1986): 292–295, at 295. Further problematically, Cowley notes a number of inaccuracies in Beylot's text.

A further important witness to the text of the *Testament* is the west Syrian *Synodicon*,[17] which, as is noted above, contains excerpts from the *Testament*. It is not, however, a complete text, and in addition rearranges some material to form canons.

Finally it should be noted that a tiny fragment of 1.23 has been discovered in Greek.[18]

Beyond these versions of the *Testament*, some prayers are found in euchologia, in Coptic and in Georgian,[19] as well as in Greek.[20] It is hard to assess the value of these prayers as witnesses to the text of the *Testament* as, although it is possible that there is a direct debt, it is also possible that these sources are drawing on a euchological tradition common to the *Testament*, rather than being directly dependent upon the *Testament*. Thus, for instance, although Chronz and Brakmann, in their presentation of the Georgian texts, point to the common occurrence of some phrases in *Testament* 1.23 and in two prayers from the Euchologion of the White Monastery, which ask that the communion about to be made does not lead to judgment or condemnation, these phrases also appear in P.Lit. Lond. 232 verso,[21] in the liturgy of John Chrysostom, and indeed are echoed in the *Acts*

[17]Vööbus, ed., *Synodicon*. The *Testament* material is in the first volume (1975), part 1, 1–49 (Syriac text), part 2, 27–64 (English translation).

[18]Simon Corcoran and Benet Salway, "A newly identified Greek fragment of the *Testamentum Domini*," *Journal of Theological Studies* 62 (2011): 118–135. Sadly it is too small to be useful in the construction of the text.

[19]The Coptic prayers are to be found in the Euchologium of the White monastery; see E. Lanne, ed., *Le grand euchologe du Monastère Blanc*, PO 28.2 (Turnhout: Brepols, 1958). In addition note that there is a Coptic version of the mystagogy. See O. Burmeister, "The Coptic and Arabic versions of the Mystagogia," Le *Muséon* 46 (1933): 203–235. On the Georgian see T. Chronz and H. Brakmann, "Fragmente des Testamentum Domini in georgischer Übersetzung," *Zeitschrift für antikes Christentum* 13 (2009): 395–402 and also Michael Kohlbacher, "Georgische Paralleltexte zum *Testament unseres Herrn Jesus Christus* (CPG 1743)," in *Akten des 5. Symposiums zur Sprache, Geschichte, Theologie und Gegenwartslage der syrischen Kirchen (V. Deutsche Syrologentagung) Berlin 14.–15. Juli 2006*, ed. Rainer M. Voigt (Aachen: Shaker, 2010), 97–126.

[20]B. Gain, "Fragments grecs inédits du Testamentum Domini attribués à Saint Basile," *Augustinianum* 32 (1992): 261–277.

[21]Jürgen Hammerstaedt, ed., *Griechische Anaphorenfragmente aus Ägypten und Nubia* (Opladen: Westdeutscher, 1999), 50–51. An English version may be found in my *Two Early Egyptian Liturgical Papyri: The Deir Balyzeh Papyrus and the Barcelona*

of Thomas![22] Oddly enough, there are echoes of the Testament in Greek in the *Liturgy of St Mark*,[23] but these are found in the *Testament* not in eucharistic material, but in the dawn hymns of 1.26. Moreover, these prayer texts are themselves "living literature" and so rework the material that may be derived from the *Testament* (or otherwise drawn from the common fund of material). Thus the blessing of oil of the *Testament* becomes a blessing of oil and water in the Georgian version published by Chronz and Brakmann. As such, although these liturgical echoes are interesting in that they potentially point to the wider and later distribution of the *Testament* (or a common set of prayer material), they are limited in their value in reconstructing the text.[24] In particular, this euchological material tends to support my hypothesis advanced elsewhere that prayer material formed a common fund that might be drawn on in different contexts.[25]

As such, it is clear that the Syriac version translated here cannot claim to be the final word on the text of *Testamentum Domini*. That would require, at the very least, a proper critical edition of the Arabic versions. However, the very fact that it is possible to identify these fragments and possible citations with reference to Rahmani's Syriac text indicates that this text is a reliable indicator of the main lines of the *Testament* and largely a faithful rendition of the Greek original.

3: The Sources and Redaction of the Testament

Certainly *Testamentum Domini* is a composite document. In particular we may recognize the *Apostolic Tradition* lying behind much of

Papyrus with Appendices Containing Comparative Material, Joint Liturgical Studies 70 (Norwich: Hymns Ancient and Modern, 2010).

[22] *Acts of Thomas* 29, 50.

[23] These are found in the prayer before the Lord's Prayer. See G. J. Cuming, *The Liturgy of St. Mark*, Orientalia Christiana Analecta 234 (Rome: Edizioni Orientalia Christiana, 1990), 50, 138.

[24] The possible exception to this is the Greek material edited by Gain "Fragments grecs." This is more extensive than the other short citations, and although there has been some expansion, one or other of these witnesses is often close to the Syriac. Some reference is had to these witnesses in the notes ad loc.

[25] In my *Two Early Egyptian Liturgical Papyri.*

the document. We may secondly readily identify the opening apocalypse, as this, as will be shown, has independent existence beyond the *Testament*. For the rest, we cannot be sure what is the work of the redactor and what further sources were employed and incorporated, though an exploration of the question may cast light on the origin and purpose of the *Testament*. In addition, it is important to be able to distinguish the work of the redactor from his sources, in particular to understand his use of *Apostolic Tradition*, in order to appreciate the value of the *Testament* for the history of liturgy.[26]

3.1: The Opening Apocalypse

The apocalypse with which the *Testament* opens is certainly an independent production for, beyond the setting of this apocalypse in the *Testament,* a clearly related apocalypse is extant in a collection of material prefixed to the Ethiopic version of *The Letter of the Apostles*.[27] Beyond this there is a fragment in Latin, containing the description of the son of perdition and of signs accompanying his coming,[28] and a distinct Syriac version.[29] I have argued

[26]Thus Rahmani, *Testamentum,* xli–xlviii, wished to assign an early date to the *Testament* largely on the basis of evidence that proved, in fact, to be material derived from *Apostolic Tradition*. By contrast, James Cooper and Arthur J. Maclean, *The Testament of Our Lord* (Edinburgh: T&T Clark, 1902), show great perspicacity in distinguishing the work of the redactor they call the "Testament compiler"; their conclusions are largely borne out by subsequent textual discoveries relating to *Apostolic Tradition*.

[27]L. Guerrier and S. Grébaut, eds., *Le Testament en Galilée de Notre Seigneur Jésus-Christ*, PO 9.3 (Paris: Firmin-Didot, 1913). The *Letter of the Apostles* is a second-century Asian work.

[28]M.R. James, ed., *Apocrypha Anecdota: A Collection of Thirteen Apocryphal Books and Fragments* (Cambridge: Cambridge UP, 1893), 151–154.

[29]J. P. Arendzen, ed., "A new Syriac text of the apocalyptic part of the 'Testament of the Lord,'" *Journal of Theological Studies* 2 (1901): 401–416. The same text was taken from a citation by Moses bar-Kepha and edited by F. Nau ("Fragment inedit d'une traduction syriaque jusqu'ici inconnue du Testamentum D.N. Jesu Christi," *Journal Asiatique* 17 [1901]: 233–256) from two Parisian manuscripts entirely independently. Although we cannot altogether exclude the possibility that this is an independent translation of *Testamentum Domini*, the independent transmission of the apocalypse would predispose us to suggest that this is a further independent exemplar.

elsewhere that this apocalypse is a product of the mid-third century and reflects events related to the Sassanian invasion of the eastern Roman Empire.[30] It thus stood ready for the redactor to incorporate into the church order that *he* was constructing. The advantage of dating the apocalypse independently is that it provides a date before which the *Testament* might not have come about. However, since the internal material of the *Testament* indicates a date rather later than the mid-third century in any event, this does not provide much assistance.

Nonetheless we may inquire whether there was any particular reason why the redactor might pick this apocalypse to preface his work. A possible clue may lie in the similarities noted between Philostorgius' description of the chaos of the Hun invasions of the eastern Empire in the closing years of the fourth century,[31] especially in the devastation of Pamphylia, Lycia, and Phrygia, and the apocalypse. These parallels have led to attempts to attribute the apocalypse to this period.[32] Such attempts have failed because it is difficult to match up the details of the apocalypse regarding emperors and rulers in east and west with the historical events of the time. However, for those living through such events, seeing them as the judgment of God,[33] the details may have been less significant than the sense that the events described (and seen as foretold) were coming to fruition in their experience, with chaotic leadership in both western and eastern empires, and so such an (already circulating) apocalypse might well be read and recycled. A renewed attempt to restore the church, and the lives of Christians, in holiness might well

[30] "The Apocalyptic Section of *Testamentum Domini*: An Attempt at Dating," *Journal of Theological Studies* 62 (2011): 136–143.

[31] Philostorgius, *Ecclesiastical History* 11.8.

[32] Notably by Arendzen, "New Syriac Text" and Joseph Bidez, *Philostorgius Kirchengeschichte*, 3rd ed. (Berlin: Akademie, 1981), cxi–cxix. This position is criticized by Bruno Bleckmann, "Apokalypse und kosmische Katastrophen: das Bild der theodosianischen Dynastie beim Kirchenhistoriker Philostorg," in *Endzeiten: Eschatologie in den monotheistischen Weltreligionen*, ed. Wolfram Brandes and Felicitas Schmieder (Berlin: de Gruyter, 2008), 13–40, at 17.

[33] As does Philostorgius, *Ecclesiastical History* 11.7.

be a response to the feeling of crisis, and occasion the recycling of this apocalypse and its attachment to a church order. Thus we may be aware of the possibility that pre-existing material might be formed into a church order by prefacing it with this apocalypse in the context of the late fourth century.

3.2: Apostolic Tradition

As has already been observed, we may also readily identify the *Apostolic Tradition,* a church order from third-century Rome,[34] as a fundamental source for the redactor's work. In particular, the order of *Apostolic Tradition* is followed closely from the chapter on the ordination of bishops, prior to which we have the apocalypse and directions regarding the church building (for which there is no Hippolytean parallel), and it is followed through to the end of the work.

In employing this source the redactor of the *Testament* has employed what may be called a layering technique. Thus the order of the source is retained, and layered with his own material. So his use begins at 1.21, with a version of *Apostolic Tradition* 2–3, containing some directions for appointment and the ordination prayer. However, this is preceded by a chapter not found in *Apostolic Tradition* that lays down qualifications. After this there is a chapter on the bishop's duties (1.22), which is not dependent on *Apostolic Tradition*, and then, in 1.23, *Apostolic Tradition* 4 is picked up and expanded. 1.24 and 1.25 are versions of *Apostolic Tradition* 5 and 6. Then *Testament* 1.26–1.28 is all new material, with *Apostolic Tradition* 7 picked up again at 1.29. The parallels are shown in the table below. Hopefully enough has been said already, however, to demonstrate the layering technique employed. The one oddity is the inclusion of *Apostolic Tradition* 38, with the omission of 37 and 39, in the middle of *Testament* 2.10, out of sequence. The omission of 37 and 39, which are short chapters related to 38, may simply be a process

[34]So, at least, I argue in my *Hippolytus: On the Apostolic Tradition*, 2nd ed. (Crestwood, NY: St Vladimir's Seminary Press, 2015). The point is, however, disputed.

of abbreviation, and it is possible that a page was misplaced, leading to this single disruption.

This manner of using a source, by following its order carefully, and interspersing other material whilst leaving the source intact, is not unusual in the ancient world. It probably originated as a result of the necessity of copying from rolls, with the attendant difficulties in combining multiple sources, but having become a normal literary procedure, it seems to have continued even after rolls were abandoned in favour of the codex.

Although there are exceptions, such as minor replacements of material and clarifications in the original, I hope to show that a similar layering technique has been employed not only in the macrostructure but also within the chapters and topics. This is significant because, once *Apostolic Tradition* material is removed, the remaining material may have its own integrity and may give us insights into the practice of the community of the redactor. In other words I hope to show that the redactor has not simply expanded *Apostolic Tradition* but has, by and large, created the *Testament* by combining *Apostolic Tradition* with another source, that this source reflects the liturgy and church structure of the redactor, and that it can be reconstructed with reasonable confidence.

3.2.1: THE EPISCOPAL ORDINATION PRAYER

As an initial example we may take the episcopal ordination prayer of 1.21. In general this prayer follows the same structure as that which lies behind *Apostolic Tradition,* and is clearly based on it, at times following it closely and yet expanding certain statements:

Thus we may compare:

> . . . and have not left your sanctuary without ministers, from the foundation of the world you were well pleased to be glorified in those you have chosen. Even now pour out from yourself the power of the Spirit of governance, which you gave to your beloved child Jesus Christ, which he gave to the holy apostles,

> who set up the church in every place as your sanctuary, for the unceasing glory and praise of your name. (*Apostolic Tradition*)

with:

> Lord God, *you have not left your exalted sanctuary without ministry since before the foundation of the world* and have, since the foundation of the world, adorned and glorified your sanctuary with faithful princes and priests after the likeness of your own heavens. You, Lord, *are pleased to be praised even now,* and have granted that there should be princes for your people. Give illumination, *pour forth* understanding and *the grace of your governing spirit which you passed on to your beloved son Jesus Christ.* Give wisdom, O God, give reason, fortitude, strength, unity in the Spirit in doing all things working with you. Grant your Spirit, holy God, which was given to your holy one, *sending it on your holy and pure church and on every place which sings of your holiness.* And grant, Lord, that this your servant should please you in *telling of your glory, in unceasing praise,* O God, in fitting hymns of glorification and in suitable occasions . . . (*Testament of the Lord*, with *Apostolic Tradition* material shown in italics)

Thus what will emerge as a key theme of the *Testament*, the mirroring of heaven in the church,[35] is introduced, and we may note that it is the bishop, rather than the church as a whole, who is to sing unceasing praise (again, the significance of this will emerge below). But although there are expansions, the structure and wording of the original are manifest in this prayer, thus demonstrating the layering technique employed by the redactor.

But what is also noteworthy about the episcopal ordination is that this prayer is the second of two. A shorter ordination prayer, said by all the bishops rather than one chosen from among those present,

[35]On which see G. Sperry-White, "The Imagery of Angelic Praise and Heavenly Topography in the *Testament of our Lord*," *Ecclesia orans* 19 (2002): 315–332.

and with all the bishops laying hands on the candidate, precedes this derivation from *Apostolic Tradition*:

> We lay hands upon a servant of God who has been elected in the Spirit for the firm and devoted ordering of the church whose headship is united and indissoluble, the invisible living God, for the delivery of true judgment and of divine and sacred revelations, and of divine gifts and of faithful teaching of the Trinity by means of the cross, by means of the resurrection, by means of the incorruption, in the sacred church of God.

Thus there are effectively two ordination prayers. Is it not possible that, beyond expanding the prayer derived from *Apostolic Tradition*, the redactor has also included the ordination prayer known in that community? We may note that, according to this prayer, the new bishop is to give revelations; we note below that the prophetic spirit is valued in the community of the *Testament*, and on this basis suggest that this first ordination prayer is certainly the ordination prayer recognized in this community. The ordination rite is expanded and supplemented in the production of the *Testament* through the addition of expanded Hippolytean material, but left intact nonetheless. We may thus, further, suggest that the acclamation of the new bishop at the end of the chapter, "he is worthy," would originally have followed the first ordination prayer in the actual rite. We thus have a layered rite, as well as a layered prayer, the layered rite revealing the ritual known to the redactor.

3.2.2: THE ANAPHORA

We may ask whether the same is true of the episcopal anaphora used at the ordination. It clearly includes material from *Apostolic Tradition*, but there is much else besides. According to Jasper and Cuming, "the *Testamentum* has simply expanded Hippolytus to double the original length by inserting two lengthy new passages."[36]

[36]R. C. D. Jasper, G. J. Cuming, *Prayers of the Eucharist: Early and Reformed*, 3rd ed. (Collegeville, MN: Liturgical Press, 1990), 138.

However, we shall note that this is far from a complete description of the redactor's procedure, and that something more substantial has taken place than the expansions exhibited by the redactor in editing the episcopal ordination prayer.

We may initially note that, although the anaphora is a clear witness to *Apostolic Tradition*, and is found in a comparable position, it is layered with material of a different origin, and surrounded by much extraneous material derived from the practice of the community of the *Testament,* in which it is made clear that this is not simply the offering of the Eucharist at an episcopal ordination as in *Apostolic Tradition*, but at a regular eucharistic celebration of the community. Apart from the introductory directions, there is a diaconal proclamation, directions regarding the reception of communion, and a post-communion prayer, none of which derive from the model.

The anaphora itself begins with a greatly expanded version of the initial thanksgiving from *Apostolic Tradition.* This is followed by an ascription of praise addressed to the Son, in which there is nothing from *Apostolic Tradition,* and an ascription of praise to the Father, in the course of which *Apostolic Tradition* is picked up again. *Apostolic Tradition* is then recognizable through the words of institution and the anamnesis and oblation. However, this is followed by a further oblation addressed to the Trinity and a prayer for the hallowing of the gifts, which dovetails into an intercession. At the end of the intercession, *Apostolic Tradition* supplies the concluding section.

We may demonstrate the use of *Apostolic Tradition* in the *Testament's* anaphora thus (Hippolytean material again being shown in italics):

> We render thanks to you, O God, who are holy, the strengthener of our souls, and giver of grace, treasury of incorruption and Father of your only begotten our savior, *whom in these recent times you have sent to us as savior and proclaimer of your purpose.* For it is your purpose that we should be saved in you. Our heart gives thanks to you Lord, our mind, our soul with all

its understanding, so that your grace may come upon us, Lord, so that we may praise you ceaselessly, and your only begotten Son and the Holy Spirit, now and for ever and to the age of the ages. Amen.

You are the strength of the Father, the grace of the nations, knowledge, true wisdom, the lifting-up of the lowly, the healing of the soul, the confidence of us who are faithful, for you are the strength of the righteous, the hope of those who are persecuted, the haven of those who are afflicted, the enlightener of the perfect, the Son of the living God. From your gifts of immeasurable greatness cause courage, fortitude, confidence, wisdom, constancy, unswerving faith, unfailing hope, knowledge of your spirit, lowliness, uprightness, to shine forth upon us, so that we your servants and all your people may always glorify you in purity, may bless you, may give thanks to you, Lord, at all times, and entreat you.

You, Lord, are the founder of the heights, the king of the treasury of lights, the overseer of the heavenly Sion, the king of the ranks of archangels, of dominions, of praises, of thrones, of clothing, of lights, of rejoicings, of delights, you who hold all things in your hand, who sustain all things in your reason, through your only begotten Son who was crucified for our sins. *You, Lord, sent your Word, Son of your mind and Son of your statute, by whom you made all that is, with whom you were well pleased, into a virgin womb. He was seen as your son, conceived and enfleshed, when he was born of the Holy Spirit and the virgin. Fulfilling your will and preparing a holy people he opened his hands for suffering so that he might set free from suffering and from corruption and death those who put their hope in you. When he was handed over to voluntary suffering so that he might set upright those who had slipped, and find those who were lost, and give life to the dead, and dissolve death, and unbind the chains of the devil, and complete the Father's will, and tread down Sheol, and open the way of life, and guide the righteous to light, and to fix a boundary, and illuminate the darkness, and increase the children, and show forth the resurrection, then he took bread. He gave it to his disciples and said: "Take, eat. This is my body, which is broken for you for the forgiveness of sins. Whenever you do this you make my memorial." Likewise the cup of wine, which he mixed, he gave as a type of the blood which was shed for us.*

Thus remembering your death and resurrection we offer to you bread and cup as we give thanks to you. You alone are God forever, and savior to us, because you have made us worthy to stand before you and to minister to you as a priest. On this account we your servants give thanks to you, Lord.

To you do we offer this thanksgiving, eternal Trinity, O Lord Jesus Christ, O Lord the Father, from whom every creature and every nature escapes into itself in trembling. O Lord *the Holy Spirit*: send some of your holiness onto this drink and this food, cause that it should not be for our condemnation, nor for our reproach, nor for our destruction, but for the healing and strengthening of our spirit. Grant, Lord, through your name, that every thought should flee which is not pleasing to you. Grant, Lord, that every thought of pride should be driven from us by means of your name, which is written within the faces of the gate of your holy heights, which cause Sheol to be stunned when it hears it, the depth is rent, spirits are driven away, the serpent is crushed, unbelief is banished, disobedience is subdued, anger is quieted, envy is rendered ineffective, arrogance is reproved, love of money is rooted out, vainglory is removed, pride is humbled, all cause of bitterness is driven away. So grant, Lord that our inward eyes may perceive you, praise you, glorify you, recall you, serve you, have part with you alone, Son and Word of God, to whom all things are subject. Sustain to the end those with the grace of revelation. Confirm those with the grace of healing. Give courage to those with the power of tongues.

> Keep upright those with a word of instruction. Take care of those who do your will at all times, visit the widows, assist the orphans. Remember those who have gone to rest in the faith. Grant us an inheritance with your saints, and grant us the grace of pleasing you just as they were pleasing to you. Shepherd the people in uprightness, and sanctify us all, O God. *But grant that all of those who participate and receive of your holy things may be united with you, so being filled with your Holy Spirit for the confirmation of the faith in truth that they may speak your praise forever, and to your beloved Son Jesus Christ as through him to you is praise and might, together with the Holy Spirit, forever and ever.*

If the "Hippolytean" material is removed from this prayer we have a shape of thanksgiving ("Our heart gives thanks to you, Lord, our mind, our soul with all its understanding . . .") followed by two prayers of praise, of which the second is addressed to the Son ("You are the strength of the Father . . ." and "You, Lord, are the founder of the heights . . ."), an offering with a prayer for the sanctification of the gifts, and an intercession. The result of the inclusion of the Hippolytean material, moreover, is a clear duplication of the oblation, first as it is taken from *Apostolic Tradition*:

> Thus remembering your death and resurrection we offer to you bread and cup as we give thanks to you . . .

and subsequently, in material with no Hippolytean parallel:

> To you do we offer this thanksgiving, eternal Trinity, O Lord Jesus Christ, O Lord the Father . . .

More subjective judgments may be made regarding the extent to which the Hippolytean material disrupts the flow of the prayer, but it may nonetheless be noted that without the additional material we have a coherent prayer. Thus, especially in the light of the duplication we may ask whether the redactor has layered an existing prayer with the Hippolytean material.

Something of this nature was suggested by Ligier, who notes a thematic and structural unity between the anaphora (less the Hippolytean material) and the daily prayers at 1.26. He thus suggests that the anaphora is that of *Apostolic Tradition* forced into the mould supplied by the daily prayers.[37] This is certainly possible, though in order to form the four prayer units into three (the shape of the daily prayers) he has to unite the first two units through the deletion of the doxology.[38] It is certainly possible that the daily prayer text has supplied the shape for the anaphora here, though it is also possible that they shared a common shape in any event.

Ligier also notes that the four verbs employed in the anaphora in the phrase "all your people may always glorify you in purity, may bless you, may give thanks to you, Lord, at all times, and entreat you" are the same as those employed in the people's responses in the daily prayers. This may again indicate that the daily prayers are the original model, though Ligier also notes that the same verbs are found in the same order in the exclamation of the Liturgy of John Chrysostom following on from the oblation: "We glorify you, we bless you, we give thanks to you, O Lord and we entreat you, our God."[39] In other words, whereas it is possible that the daily prayer has provided the pattern for the anaphora here, it is also possible that prayers of anaphoral origin have provided a pattern for the daily prayers. We may recollect here, moreover, that elements from the dawn hymn appear in the *Liturgy of St Mark*. The parallel with the liturgy of John Chrysostom is particularly striking since, as already

[37]Louis Ligier, "L'anaphore de la 'Tradition apostolique' dans le Testamentum Domini," in *The Sacrifice of Praise: Studies on the Themes of Thanksgiving and Redemption in the Central Prayers of the Eucharistic and Baptismal Liturgies in Honour of Arthur Hubert Couratin*, ed. B. D. Spinks, Ephemerides liturgicae, Subsidia 19 (Rome: Edizioni Liturgiche, 1981), 91–106, at 98.

[38]This is not as arbitrary as it might seem at first sight since it is found neither in the Ethiopic nor in Troupeau's Arabic text.

[39]Ligier, "Anaphore," 100–101.

observed, there is a further parallel to that anaphora in the request in the *Testament*'s anaphora that the communion does not lead to judgment or condemnation. Whether originally anaphoral prayers have been employed in the construction of daily prayer texts, or daily prayer texts employed in the construction of an anaphora, again we meet the phenomenon of prayer units with independent origins being used in the construction of further prayers.

We may also note the suggestion of Arranz that an early anaphora is hidden in this text.[40] Whilst following the same procedure of removing elements clearly derived from *Apostolic Tradition,* Arranz deduces that the *Testament* contains a primitive anaphora because of the absence of the *Sanctus* and intercessions. However, I have suggested elsewhere that the intercessions are, in the case of one line of anaphoral development at least, an integral part of the original anaphora, and that in some circles the *Sanctus* might make an early entrée.[41] We may also suggest that the section beginning "Sustain to the end those with the grace of revelation . . ." looks suspiciously like an intercession. Arranz suggests that this represents a stage of development represented by the domestic Eucharist prior to its fusion with synagogal prayers (from which the *Sanctus* made its entrée into the anaphora.) What is really problematic about this is the theory of development, derived from Bouyer,[42] which assumes that any such development took place. Bouyer's hypothesis is questionable in the extreme and has won little acceptance. Nonetheless, in spite of the failure of Arranz's version of the hypothesis, the question of

[40]Miguel Arranz, "Les rôles dans l'assemblée chrétienne d'après le 'Testamentum Domini,'" in *L'Assemblée liturgique et les différents roles dans l'Assemblée* (Rome: Edizioni liturgiche, 1977), 43–77, at 46.

[41]In "*Catecheses mystagogicae* 5 and the Birkath HaMazon: A Study in Development," *Augustinianum* 45 (2005): 309–349. We should also note Baumstark's suggestion in "Arabischen Texte," 298, that the text of the *Sanctus* was recited by the bishop where the Syriac versions now have "holy things." This is now supported by Troupeau's Arabic version. I have retained the Syriac version, though without complete conviction.

[42]Louis Bouyer, *Eucharist: Theology and Spirituality of the Eucharistic Prayer* (Notre Dame, IN: University of Notre Dame, 1968), 91–135.

whether an anaphora is to be found beneath this text is one clearly worth pursuing. Certainly the duplication of the offering gives rise to a suspicion that two anaphoras have been joined together by the incorporation of the anaphora of *Apostolic Tradition* into an earlier anaphora.

If we accept that the shape of this hypothetical anaphora is that of a thanksgiving, followed by prayers of praise, an offering to the Trinity with a prayer for the hallowing of the gifts and an intercession, we may ask if there is any parallel for such an anaphoral shape. Although the answer is that there is no precise parallel, we may note that the anaphora of *Addai and Mari* has some similarity with this. The anaphora moves similarly from thanksgiving and praise (including the *Sanctus)* to remembrance of the acts of God, turning to a brief intercession (joined to the offering) and ending with an epiclesis and doxology.

The problem with using *Addai and Mari* as a basis for any comparison is that whereas there is widespread agreement that the anaphora as it stands is the result of development from a more basic form, there is no agreement as to what that basic form might have been.[43] However, at the center of the anaphora there is a thanksgiving and oblation followed directly by intercessions (without any anamnesis, as in other classical liturgies where intercessions follow the oblation.) Thus we may compare:

Oblation: And for all thy graces towards us we offer thee glory and honour and thanksgiving and adoration now and at all times and for ever and ever.

Intercession: Do thou, O my Lord, in thy manifold mercies make a good remembrance for all the upright and just fathers, the prophets and apostles and martyrs and confessors, in the commemoration of the body and blood of thy Christ, which we

[43]For discussion see Stephen B. Wilson, "The Anaphora of the Apostles Addai and Mari," in *Essays on Early Eastern Eucharistic Prayers*, ed. Paul F. Bradshaw (Collegeville, MN: Liturgical Press, 1997), 19–37.

> offer to thee upon the pure and holy altar, as thou hast taught us in his life-giving Gospel. And make with us thy tranquillity and thy peace all the days of the age . . .[44]

to:

> **Oblation:** To you do we offer this thanksgiving, eternal Trinity, O Lord Jesus Christ, O Lord the Father, from whom every creature and every nature escapes into itself in trembling.
>
> **Intercession:** Grant, Lord, through your name, that every thought should flee which is not pleasing to you . . .

Thus there is a common movement from thanksgiving to intercession, and a common pattern of thanksgiving and praise as the dominant notes of both anaphoras. Moreover, in common with the hypothetical anaphora of the *Testament*, there is an address to the Trinity, and some lack of clarity in the address to the Father and the Son similar to that found in the *Testament*. This will be explored below, but we may now agree with Botte that the phenomenon in *Addai and Mari* reflects a primitive Trinitarian theology,[45] and may observe now that the same is the case in the *Testament*. What is also particularly interesting, in the light of Ligier's suggestion with regard to the *Testament*, is the possibility that *Addai and Mari* itself originated in a daily prayer-form.[46] In other words, the similarity may come about because neither has developed from table prayers but rather are both outgrowths from daily praise. There are, moreover, differences; in particular the epiclesis is in a different place, following the intercessions in *Addai and Mari*, and preceding them in the *Testament*. However, it is also possible that the epiclesis of *Addai and*

[44]From the Anaphora of *Addai and Mari* as translated by A. Gelston, *The Eucharistic Prayer of Addai and Mari* (Oxford: Clarendon, 1992), here at 121.

[45]See particularly B. Botte, "L'Anaphore *Chaldéen* des Apôtres," *Orientalia Christiana Periodica* 15 (1949): 259–276.

[46]B. D. Spinks, "The Original Form of the Anaphora of the Apostles: A Suggestion in the Light of the Maronite Sharar," *Ephemerides liturgicae* 91 (1977): 146–161, at 150–152.

Mari is a later addition to the text,[47] the removal of which would conform the shape of the two anaphoras more closely.

In summary, we note that while the text of the anaphora of *Apostolic Tradition* is largely preserved, it is extensively expanded through layering in such a way that it must be counted as a recasting rather than simply a translation and, more significantly, may incorporate an anaphora employed in the community of the *Testament*, made up of multiple prayer units, giving praise, making the offering, and joining intercession to the act of oblation. As an alternative understanding it is also possible that the redactor has simply worked euchological material familiar to him (rather than simply a prayer) into the structure provided by *Apostolic Tradition*, though if this is the case it is hard to perceive by what principles he worked. Thus it seems more probable that two anaphoras, one from *Apostolic Tradition*, the other traditional in the community of the *Testament*, have been combined.

3.2.3: THE BLESSING OF OIL

In *Apostolic Tradition* the anaphora is followed by blessings for oil and for cheese and olives. The *Testament* similarly has prayer for the blessing of oil in this position, but the prayer bears little resemblance to those of *Apostolic Tradition* apart from a reference to the "type of fatness," which is found in *Apostolic Tradition*'s prayer over the olives. Perhaps more significantly, the prayers make it clear that the oil is for anointing, for healing, and for penitents in a way that is less clear than it is in *Apostolic Tradition*. Indeed, it is a point of interest that the anointing of penitents is envisaged in this community. Here, we may suggest, material native to the *Testament*'s community has been worked into the structure provided by the original, in this case leaving little of the original behind.

[47] On this point I follow J. Magne, "L'anaphore nestorienne dite d'Addée et Mari et l'anaphore maronite dite de Pierre III: étude comparative," *OCP* 53 (1987): 107–159, at 145–147. The epiclesis here separates a string of participles from their governing verb.

3.2.4: THE CATECHUMENAL AND BAPTISMAL RITUALS

The baptismal rite described in the *Testament* likewise clearly manifests the redactor's layering technique. The greater part of the ritual is largely derived from *Apostolic Tradition.* However, there are some significant additions and deviations.

First, we may note the following:

> As he takes hold of each of them he should ask, as the one being baptized turns towards the west, he should say: "Say: 'I renounce you Satan, and all your service, and your pomps, and your pleasures, and all your works.'"

The exorcistic pre-baptismal anointing follows, and then we read:

> And turning him to the east he should say: "I submit to you, Father and Son and Holy Spirit, before whom all nature trembles and is moved. Grant that I may blamelessly do your will."

This may be compared to the (reconstructed) text of *Apostolic Tradition*:

> And when the presbyter takes hold of each of those who are to be baptized he should bid him renounce saying: "I renounce you, Satan, and all your service and all your works." And when he has renounced all this he should anoint him with the oil of exorcism saying to him: "Let all evil spirits depart far from you."

Apostolic Tradition then proceeds directly to the baptismal rite.

We may note the slightly extended form of renunciation and the more detailed form of exorcism in the *Testament* (omitted here on grounds of length), but what is really significant is the turning of the candidate to the west at the renunciation, and then to the east, where there is the appearance of a form of commitment, known as the *syntaxis*, not found in *Apostolic Tradition.* This is more than simply an additional ritual detail, since the *syntaxis,* following the renunciation, was the fundamental baptismal profession in eastern rites, rather than the western form, which involved assent to a creed delivered whilst the candidate is in the water, which is the form of baptismal profession found in *Apostolic Tradition.* As examples we may note the (west Syrian) "western text" of Acts 8.36, where the Ethiopian eunuch asks what is to prevent him being baptized. The western text then inserts Philip's response: "If you believe with your whole heart it is possible." The Ethiopian eunuch then replies in turn: "I believe that Jesus Christ is the Son of God," and is baptized on the basis of this confession of faith. We may also note the baptismal scenes in the Syrian *History of John.* In one, the procurator, when he is baptized, asks what he is to say. John replies that he must reply in keeping with what he has come to believe. So the procurator calls out "I believe in the name of the Father and the Son and the Spirit of holiness," and so jumps into the font.[48] The priests of Ephesus similarly call out, before they are baptized, "We believe in the name of the Father and the Son and the Spirit of holiness and we will never know anything else."[49] We may also point to the practices described by John Chrysostom and Theodore of Mopsuestia[50] in which candidates make a brief confession of faith immediately prior to baptism.

After the *Testament* gives us this rite of commitment, we subsequently have a confession of faith in which the candidate assents to the creed in questioning. This repetitive procedure is not a reflection of the rite of the community of the *Testament*, I suggest, but is simply the result of including the baptismal rite of *Apostolic Tradition*; in this text, as elsewhere in the west, the candidate professes *his* faith response to questions, delivered in the water. Thus in the *Testament*

[48]W. Wright, ed., *Apocryphal Acts of the Apostles* (London: Williams and Norgate, 1871; repr., Piscataway, NJ: Gorgias, 2005), 1:44 (Syriac text), 2:40 (English translation).

[49]Wright, *Apocryphal Acts,* 1:59 (Syriac), 2:54 (English).

[50]See the homilies of these authors, most easily accessed through Edward Yarnold, *The Awe-Inspiring Rites of Initiation*, 2nd ed. (Collegeville, MN: Liturgical Press, 1994). Note in particular p. 158 (Chrysostom) and p. 170 (Theodore).

we have a composite rite, which comes about through adding the material of *Apostolic Tradition*, in which there is an acquiescence to credal questions delivered while the candidate is in the water, to an eastern rite in which the faith is confessed prior to baptism and after the renunciation. The result is a duplication of the candidates' statement of belief.

Evidence that, as elsewhere, the assent is the basic credal declaration, is found in a slight recasting of a rubric in the original regarding the necessity of allowing no alien object into the water. Whereas *Apostolic Tradition* reads: "... after they have let down their hair and laid down the gold and silver ornaments which they have on them ..." the *Testament* has: "When those who are being baptized go down (to the water), after they have responded and spoken, the bishop should see lest any of them, any man having a gold ring, or a woman having any gold (ornament) upon her person." The critical words here are "after they have responded and spoken." That is to say the baptismal response that is critical in this community is the *syntaxis*, which precedes baptism in water, rather than any response which takes place while the candidate is in the water.

Although I have suggested that the *Testament* describes a composite rite, it might be objected that such a composite rite is not necessarily a literary fiction, and that such a composite rite might actually have been practised. A similarly composite rite appears in Jerusalem, in the *Mystagogical Catecheses*. There the renunciation and the *syntaxis* are described, much as in the *Testament*: the candidate faces west and renounces Satan, his works, his pomp, and his service, and then, facing east, is bidden to say: "I believe in the Father and in the Son and in the Holy Spirit and in one baptism of repentance." All this takes place in the antechamber. Then, when the candidate(s) come to the pool we hear: "And each one was asked if he believed in the name of the Father and of the Son and of the Holy Spirit. You professed this saving confession and you descended three times into the water and ascended again."[51]

[51] *Mystagogical Catecheses* 1.9; 2.4; St Cyril of Jerusalem, *Lectures on the Christian*

We may suggest that this has come about due to the peculiar situation of Jerusalem, as a meeting point for various liturgical practices. It is unlikely that the community of the Testament was similarly exposed to such variety. Rather the composite rite found there is purely a literary product, the result of layering an existing, eastern, rite with that of *Apostolic Tradition*.

Secondly, after the presbyteral post-baptismal anointing, we read:

> Women, however, should be anointed by the widows who are seated foremost, while the presbyter speaks over them. At baptism also these widows who are veiled should receive them under a veil, while the bishop says these professions. And thus also while he speaks to them of the things they are to renounce.

The practice of having the widows anoint the female candidates is reminiscent of the *Didascalia of the Apostles*,[52] in which deaconesses anoint female candidates; the practice of using widows may well be that from which the practice of the *Didascalia* had developed. Indeed, I have already suggested that the office of female deacon in the Didascalist community had come about to bring women under tighter episcopal control, in view of the relative independence of the order of widows.[53] The anointing by widows, and the veiling, is undertaken as a result of the nudity of the candidates. What is also noteworthy, however, is that the pre-baptismal anointing is also

Sacraments: The Protocatechesis and the Five Mystagogical Catecheses Ascribed to St Cyril of Jerusalem, trans. Maxwell E. Johnson, Popular Patristics Series 57 (Yonkers, NY: St Vladimir's Seminary Press, 2017), 93, 99.

[52]The *Didascalia* is another church order text. Although its latest level of redaction is, I have suggested, in the middle of the fourth century, it may have earlier layers. See my *The Didascalia Apostolorum: An English Version* (Turnhout: Brepols, 2009).

[53]It is interesting to note that deaconesses make occasional appearance in the *Testament* but are clearly junior in the hierarchy. They receive communion before other women but after all others (1.23), and are classed with the readers and subdeacons in the deacon's litany (1.35), and are to be trained by the widows (1.40). The only liturgical duty attributed to them is to carry communion to women who are sick (2.20).

carried out by widows. This indicates that, like the pre-baptismal anointing to which Chrysostom and Theodore bear witness, it is not an anointing of the head only but of the whole body.

There are questions that remain unanswered, in particular with regard to the anointings. The pre-baptismal anointing in *Apostolic Tradition* is clearly exorcistic, and the expanded form that the *Testament* gives implies that this is likewise the understanding in this community, as opposed to the east Syrian pre-baptismal anointing that is intended to convey the Holy Spirit. We may, moreover, note Bradshaw's suggestion that the east Syrian and west Syrian pre-baptismal anointings are distinct not only in this understanding, but in that the west Syrian practice was always an anointing of the body, as it would seem to be in the *Testament*, whereas further east the head alone was anointed.[54] However, the two post-baptismal anointings of *Apostolic Tradition* are retained, and so we cannot know the extent to which these reflect the practice of the community. The renunciations are listed separately, in the statement that widows are to assist with the anointing; the anointing at renunciation thus seems like something of an afterthought, which implies that a post-baptismal anointing is meant here. Such a statement, moreover, indicates familiarity with the practice of post-baptismal anointing; again this is west Syrian rather than east Syrian practice. We may also note here the diaconal petition that the catechumens should attain the bath of regeneration and be sanctified "with the mark of sanctification" (1.35), which again indicates knowledge of a post-baptismal anointing. All this indicates that the familiar practice of the *Testament* was a single (as opposed to a double) post-baptismal anointing. As such, this, alongside the pre-baptismal anointing of the whole body, is precisely what one would anticipate whether the *Testament* originated in Palestine, Antioch, or Asia Minor.

[54]Paul F. Bradshaw, "Women and Baptism in the *Didascalia apostolorum*," *Journal of Early Christian Studies* 20 (2012): 641–645, at 644–645.

We may finally note that the *Testament* omits any reference to the offering of milk and honey to the newly baptized. As Quasten observes, this custom is unknown in the eastern churches.[55]

The *Testament* thus tends to confirm information obtained elsewhere regarding the development of baptismal rites, once the layering of *Apostolic Tradition* is removed, but sadly supplies little that is new. Nonetheless, this is still a positive result. First, what can be discerned points to a potential mid- to late fourth-century date, and to a provenance in Asia or Palestine, but not further east. Secondly, the clear emergence of a recognizable baptismal rite, once the Hippolytean layers are removed, tends to confirm the rightness of the procedure of removing layers in order to expose an original, thus lending a greater security to any conclusions reached on the basis of such a procedure with regard to material, such as the anaphora, about which we are less well informed.

3.2.5: DAILY PRAYER

At 1.22 it is said that the bishop should "persist in prayer, day and night, especially at the required times in the night, at the first hour, in the middle of the night, and at first light when the day star appears, and again in the morning at the third hour, the sixth, the ninth, and the twelfth hour of the lamp."

At 2.24, however, a fuller *horarium* appears, based on *Apostolic Tradition*. The hours given are dawn, the third, sixth, and ninth hours, evening, midnight, and dawn again. These are the same hours as given in *Apostolic Tradition*. The justifications given are, however, somewhat abbreviated; those of the *Testament*, moreover, center entirely on the passion and resurrection. Thus whereas for *Apostolic Tradition* midnight is identified as a time at which creation pauses to praise God, in the *Testament* this is stated to be the time of the resurrection, and at the third hour the original statement that this is

[55]Johannes Quasten, "Die Ostervigil im Testamentum Domini," in *Paschatis sollemnia: Studien zu Osterfeier und Osterfrömmigkeit*, ed. Balthasar Fischer and Johannes Wagner (Basel: Herder, 1959), 87–95, at 94.

the hour of the crucifixion is maintained, even as a passage regarding the showbread is dropped. Similarly whereas *Apostolic Tradition* identifies cockcrow as the time at which Christ was betrayed, for the *Testament* this is again identified with the passion and resurrection, as it states: "because after he arose he glorified the Father while they were singing psalms." As a result it is not clear whether this hour of prayer duplicates the prayer on waking, as it does in *Apostolic Tradition*, or whether this has been formed into a distinct time of prayer, to correspond with the prayer "at first light when the daystar appears" in the earlier *horarium*.[56] Interpretation is not helped by comparison to the practice of Basil, as there is similar lack of clarity there.[57] Nonetheless the horarium that emerges is similar to that known to Basil, even though the justifications offered for the times of prayer differ. We may also note the similarities, highlighted in the notes to the translation, with the Ps.-Athanasian *On Virginity*. This text does not give an *horarium* as such, and so it is difficult to make direct comparisons, but there are a number of prayer practices in common and, as also noted in the introduction below, at a number of points similar justifications are given for prayers at particular hours.

It seems that whereas the redactor of the *Testament* has honored the original to the extent of including the chapter, the material is remodeled in order to conform this timetable to that known and recognized in the redactor's community, which in turn is also that

[56]Grant White, *Daily Prayer and Its Ascetic Context in the Syriac and Ethiopic* Testamentum Domini (Joensuu: University of Joensuu, 2002), 132, who suggests that the duplication is maintained, though P. F. Bradshaw, Maxwell E. Johnson, and L. E. Phillips, *The Apostolic Tradition: A Commentary* (Minneapolis, MN: Fortress, 2002), 212–213, believe that the underlying source (*Apostolic Tradition*) intended two distinct offices.

[57]Robert Taft, *The Liturgy of the Hours in East and West* (Collegeville, MN: Liturgical Press, 1986), 86, with reference to Basil's *horarium* at *Longer Rule* 37, believes that Basil is also referring to a single office, when the dawn office is mentioned at the beginning and the end of the *horarium*, whereas W. K. Lowther Clarke, *The Ascetic Works of Saint Basil* (London: S.P.C.K., 1925), 209n4, suggests that there are two offices on the basis that the first direction states that prayer should be at dawn *(orthros)* whereas the conclusion speaks of anticipating *(prophthasantas)* the dawn.

of the Cappadocian communities. The weight given throughout the document to the prayers that mark the day indicate that this was a primary concern of the redactor, and so, by contrast to the treatment of the baptismal rite, this concern outweighed any fidelity to the source.

3.2.6: CONCLUSION

Whereas there are parts of the *Testament* where *Apostolic Tradition* is followed closely, elsewhere material is worked into the framework provided by *Apostolic Tradition*, thus recasting the original, and elsewhere omissions and expansions construct a document entirely distinct from the original. It is where the *Testament* departs from the *Tradition* that we can most clearly discern the practice of the redactor's community. In all this we may observe a layering technique, and so identify the expansions and alterations that are clues to the redactor's intent and the practice of his community.

3.3: *The Mystagogy*

At 1.28 an extended "mystagogy" is included. This would seem to be an independent literary unit, possibly a paschal proclamation in origin, which has been incorporated into the *Testament*. Proof of this lies in the independent existence of a (Bohairic Coptic) version employed in the Coptic liturgy at the consecration of the oils.[58] Although there are broad parallels with other literature concerning Christ's descent into hell,[59] there is nothing in these parallels that either necessitates or precludes the inclusion of this piece in the primary level of redaction of the *Testament*.

It is noteworthy that there are a few phrases in the version found in the *Testament* not found in the Coptic version, such as "passible and impassible." Wordsworth claimed that these phrases indicate an Apollinarian origin to the *Testament*. However, the Coptic version

[58] Burmeister, ed., "Coptic and Arabic Versions."

[59] Jean Parisot, "Note sur la mystagogie du 'Testament du Seigneur,'" *Journal asiatique* 9.15 (1900): 377–380.

is itself not immune from doctrinal adjustments (for instance, in a clearly fifth-century touch, Christ is said to have become man unchangeably), and so we cannot use this as a witness to the text of the *Testament*. Such "corrections" may indeed imply that the absent phrases have been omitted in order to conform the mystagogy to the Orthodoxy of a later period.

Although we may include the mystagogy as an independently existing source employed by the redactor of the *Testament*, it does not cast a great deal of light on the period, the locale, or the redactional intent of the *Testament's* redactor. However, since a fourth-century and Asian origin will be suggested below, we may observe that this homiletic fragment is entirely at home in such a context. We may note in particular the elaborate Asian style of the piece. For instance we may observe the use of *ēthopoiia* (speeches in character) on the part of death personified and of Christ, the long lists of attributes such as "he is our light, salvation, savior, protector, helper, teacher, deliverer, rewarder, assistance, strength, wall. He is our shepherd, entrance, door, way, life, medicine, food, drink, judge," here combined with *asyndeton* (a lack of connectives) to increase its rhetorical effect, as well as the series of antitheses, such as "passible and impassible" (the phrase notably missing from the Coptic), "dead yet living, incomprehensible and comprehensible." All this is typical of the rhetoric of the Asian schools of the second and third centuries. Those unfamiliar with such rhetoric may readily compare the *On Pascha* of Melito. Although the existence of such rhetorical artifice does not prove that the two documents share a context, it is suggestive nonetheless. Whatever its date, the mystagogy preserves for us a gem of early Christian speech.

Its use in the Coptic rite on Maundy Thursday may even indicate an origin in a paschal setting, as may the statement of the *Testament* that it is to be delivered on Sundays and in the festal seasons. As such we may reasonably suggest that the redactor has embedded into the *Testament* a paschal *praeconium* of some antiquity that was known and employed in this community.

3.4: Other Material Distinct to the Testament

The material distinct to the *Testament* that has been examined so far all clearly derives from identifiable written sources that have independent existence beyond the *Testament*. There is other material that is distinct to the *Testament* that may derive from separate sources, or may be the free composition of the redactor. These are the instructions regarding church buildings (*Testament* 1.19), the instructions regarding the bishop, with related liturgical material (in particular prayer texts) (*Testament* 1.20, 1.22, those parts of 1.23 that are not derived from *Apostolic Tradition*, 1.26–27, and the end of 1.28), instructions regarding presbyters (again including liturgical material, in particular daily prayer texts) (*Testament* 1.29, 1.31–32), instructions regarding deacons (including liturgical material, but not daily prayer texts) (*Testament* 1.33–37), instructions regarding widows (again, including liturgical material, in particular daily prayer texts) (*Testament* 1.40–43), and miscellaneous other instructions relating to Pascha (*Testament* 2.12–20, interrupted by a chapter regarding wills and death [2.15] and some *Apostolic Tradition* material). We briefly examine this material, before seeking to see what of this might be assigned to a written source.

3.4.1: THE CHURCH BUILDING OF THE *TESTAMENT*

Although the *Testament* gives a description of a church building, with ancillary structures, it is hard to match this building with any particular archaeological evidence. Thus an attempt to align this chapter with building practice in Illyria has not met much agreement.[60] Moreover, although apparently detailed, there are some uncertainties in the description. Whereas the earliest dedicated Christian meeting places were adaptations of domestic buildings,

[60]See Paul Post, "La liturgie en tant qu'architecture?," *Bijdragen* 42 (1981): 392–420, in response to Dimitrios Pallas, "L'édifice cultuel chrétien et la liturgie dans l'Illyricum oriental," in *Eisēgēseis tou Dekatou Diethnous Sunedriou Christianikēs Archaiologoias* (Thessalonike: Société d'études macédoniennes, 1980), 497–570.

the shape of the basilica, a rectangular meeting hall, was adopted widely by Christians, particularly in the fourth century.[61] It seems that a basilica is being described, but octagonal structures were not uncommon, particularly built as *martyria*, and we cannot be sure that this is not intended here, although the fact that the baptistery is (unusually) apparently rectangular would tend to militate against this. The triple entrance is, moreover, reminiscent of Constantinian basilical models.[62]

Beyond this we may, with Kohlbacher, ask the purpose of the provisions.[63] Is this a conservative statement in some kind of response to a new style of church building, or the very opposite, a new approach introduced under the guise of tradition? Possibly the redactor is commending the use of a basilica, rather than a shape or structure derived from an adapted domestic building, or alternatively is maintaining a basilica shape against that of a *martyrium*. We cannot know, though it is likely that, given the probability that the building is a basilica, the adoption of the basilica, originating in the west of the empire, is being encouraged.[64]

The one thing we can state is that the church building is surrounded by others relating to the life of the community; again this indicates that the construction of a basilica is being recommended

[61]On the subject of the early development of church building in general, see Richard Krautheimer, *Early Christian and Byzantine Architecture*, 4th ed. (New Haven, CT: Yale University Press, 1986), 1–166; L. Michael White, *The Social Origins of Christian Architecture*, vol. 1, *Building God's House in the Roman World: Architectural Adaptation Among Pagans, Jews, and Christians* (Valley Forge, PA: Trinity, 1996).

[62]The notes to the text ad loc. point to the three gates to the east of Constantine's church of the Holy Sepulchre (Eusebius, *Life of Constantine* 3.37) and the triple entrance to the basilica at Tyre (Eusebius, *Church History* 10.4.41.)

[63]Michael Kohlbacher, "Das Kirchenbau-Kapitel des Testamentum Domini Nostri Jesu Christi," in *Architektur und Liturgie: Akten des Kolloquiums vom 25. bis 27. Juli 2003 in Greifswald*, ed. Michael Altripp and Claudia Nauerth (Wiesbaden: Ludwig Reichert, 2006), 35–38 (summary).

[64]On the adoption of the basilica, see the helpful summary of studies by Sible de Blaauw, "A Classic Question: The Origins of the Church Basilica and Liturgy," in *Costantino e i costantinidi: l'innovazione costantiniana, le sue radici e i suoi sviluppi*, ed. Olof Brandt and Gabriele Castiglia (Vatican City: Pontificio Istituto di archeologia cristiana, 2016), 553–562.

here.[65] As such this reflects the use by resident ascetics that is discussed below. The church is more than a church; it is the center of an ascetic community.

3.4.2: THE DAILY PRAYER TEXTS OF THE PEOPLE, THE PRESBYTERS, AND THE WIDOWS

As has already been noted, the presbyters of the *Testament* are bound to a cycle of daily prayer. It has also been noted that the *Testament* adapts the *horarium* of *Apostolic Tradition* in such a way that it seems that a native *horarium* has been superimposed upon the original. This in itself points up the significance of daily prayer to the redactor. Indeed, large amounts of the work are given over to the texts employed, and particular forms of daily prayer are given for the people (led by the bishop),[66] the presbyters, and the widows, each of which falls into the same threefold shape. It is noteworthy that the presbyters and bishop, as well as the widows, are said to be constant in prayer, in contrast to the Hippolytean source. Thus we can reasonably state that the practice of daily prayer is of the utmost importance to the community of the *Testament*.

These prayer texts and provisions have been subjected to a detailed study by White, who concludes that these texts derive from an ascetic community, in particular observing parallels from the Cappadocian Ps.-Athanasian *On Virginity*. Thus he notes parallels between the *horaria* of the two documents,[67] the manner in which *On Virginity* 14 knows of senior women who exercise authority in their ascetic communities (suggesting that the presbyters and widows play a similar role in this community),[68] and the manner in which the bishop and widows of the *Testament* are encouraged

[65] Eusebius, *Church History* 10.4.41, refers to the outbuildings and side-rooms of the basilica of Tyre.

[66] This, however, is not necessarily daily, but was a preliminary office to the Eucharist, which was not a daily celebration. See, for discussion, White, *Daily Prayer*, 136–145.

[67] White, *Daily Prayer*, 127–129; likewise Taft, *Liturgy of the Hours*, 88–89.

[68] White, *Daily Prayer*, 47, 98.

to have those around them who are like-minded,[69] in common with the provisions of *On Virginity* 10. It is further worth noting White's comment on the widows' dawn prayers that they speak with the "vocabulary of the Christian ascetic struggle."[70] As already noted, this is an indication of some form of prior and independent existence for the material. We may also note with him the manner in which the description of presbyters' duties forms a coherent literary unit,[71] again indicating prior and independent existence of this material.

Beyond the *horarium*, given for the bishop and the people, the prayer texts for presbyters and widows show distinct concerns. Thus the presbyter is to pray "each at his own occasion," which, White suggests, means that each of the (twelve) presbyters is to pray at some hour of day or night so that prayer is continuous.[72] The widows' prayers are specifically enjoined "at the appointed times, by herself, during the night (and) at dawn."[73] The texts given then relate to these occasions, namely the night and the dawn. This is closely paralleled by the Ps.-Athanasian *On Virginity* 20: "In the middle of the night, you shall awake and hymn the Lord your God, because at this hour our Lord arose from the dead and hymned his Father . . . just before dawn say this psalm: 'O God, my God, I rise early for you, my soul thirsts for you,' then, at daybreak, 'Bless all the works of the Lord, sing praise to the Lord.'" The Ps.-Athanasian work provides psalmody, as opposed to the hymnody of the *Testament*, but the significant point is that the offering of prayer at these times is common practice for ascetic women.

The *Testament* is unique among the church orders in its inclusion of these complete prayer texts. Their inclusion, and the distinct emphases of the different groups within the church, represent a form of asceticism akin to that known from the correspondence

[69] 1.2, 1.40, 1.42.
[70] White, *Daily Prayer*, 80.
[71] White *Daily Prayer*, 94.
[72] White, *Daily Prayer*, 90.
[73] *Testament* 1.42.

and ascetic directions of Basil the Great, and even more the Ps.-Athanasian work, as the practice of spirituality grows into the life of the Church.

3.4.3: THE PASCHAL PROVISIONS OF THE *TESTAMENT*

As has already been noted, interspersed with material from *Apostolic Tradition* are a number of provisions regarding Pascha. Extensive reading with psalmody and hymnody is decreed, and provision is made for baptism at this paschal vigil.[74] Although the springboard for this is a discussion of Pascha in *Apostolic Tradition*, the material included is entirely distinct.[75] Provision is also made for the bishop and ascetics to extend the vigil until dawn, whereas others are dismissed at midnight with the conclusion of the Eucharist. Again this speaks to the ascetic orientation of this community.

One provision is of particular interest, namely that babies should be kept awake. Strobel suggests that this is in view of the eschatological expectation attached to the Pascha, which may in turn be an indication of an originally Quartodeciman understanding of the Pascha as the occasion for the parousia.[76] This does not assist, however, with the literary riddle of the *Testament*'s construction, though once again it is an indication of an Asian milieu.

3.4.4: THE DUTIES AND QUALIFICATIONS OF THE BISHOP, PRESBYTERS, AND DEACONS OF THE *TESTAMENT*

Although the skeleton of the chapters on bishop, presbyters, and deacons may be that of *Apostolic Tradition*, much of the material is entirely independent. In particular we may point to the criteria for selection for these orders, and the description of their duties, as well

[74]*Testament* 2.12, 18–20. Note that the provision for baptism is already present here, and so duplicates the material from *Apostolic Tradition*.

[75]Cf. the treatment of Quasten, "Ostervigil," who treats less of the actual paschal material here than of the baptismal material, which is largely drawn from *Apostolic Tradition*.

[76]August Strobel, *Ursprung und Geschichte des frühchristlichen Osterkalenders* (Berlin: Akademie, 1977), 39.

as the liturgical material such as the deacon's proclamation on the Eucharist that appears at 1.35.

What is particularly to be noted, in keeping with the overall ascetic orientation of the *Testament* and the insight of White, already mentioned, is that the presbyters seem less to be an order of ministry with congregational duties (as elsewhere in the church order tradition) than a cadre of older men devoted to prayer, in that the duties of the presbyter, beyond the maintenance of the life of prayer and fasting, seem principally to be in the direction of ascetics. Thus White points out the extent to which the vocabulary of this section mirrors that of Evagrius.[77] The presbyter is to examine those who hear the word for signs of *askēsis* and negative dispositions that, in Evagrian terms, are to stir up the passions.

By contrast it is the deacon who, rather than being a bishop's officer (though this is found in *Testament* 1.34, derived from *Apostolic Tradition*), has the pastoral task both of keeping discipline within the church and in caring for the congregation in the wider community. We may suggest that it reflects the realities of the *Testament* community, that is to say, the presbyters form an ascetic cadre, whereas the deacons exercise the daily ministry of the church. This in turn makes it less likely that the discussion of deacons' duties is derived from a written source, but is rather the elaboration and extension by the redactor of a brief passage on this matter in *Apostolic Tradition*.

In part this comes about because the bishop's office is likewise ascetized. Thus all that is said of the bishop's duties pertains to his life of prayer (being constantly by the altar) and fasting.[78] Thus whereas White suggests that there is a fusion of two traditions of order, namely a church order based on the bishop and one based on the senior men and women of the community, who form the ascetic cadre,[79] we may suggest rather that such a church order reflects the conditions widespread in earlier centuries, particularly in Asia,

[77]White, *Daily Prayer*, 92–98.
[78]*Testament* 1.22.
[79]White, Daily Prayer, 155–156.

in which ministry was the task of bishops and deacons, whereas presbyters formed a cadre of patrons.[80] It has been transformed, however, through the formation of the presbyterate into an ascetic, rather than patronal, group and the alignment of the bishop with this ascetic group.

We may also examine the qualifications laid down for the various offices. In the directions concerning the selection of bishops we read:

> He should be faultless, chaste, gentle, humble, free of anxiety, watchful, not a lover of money, blameless, not contentious, merciful, learned, not talkative, a lover of what is good, a lover of labor, a lover of the widows, a lover of the orphans, a lover of the poor, who is familiar with the mysteries, not lax or fond of this world's company, who is peaceable, perfect in all that is good, as one to whom the position and the place of God is entrusted. It is good if he is without wife, but should at least be the husband of one wife so that he may sympathize with the weakness of the widows. When he is appointed he should be of middle age, not a youth.[81]

Nearly all of these qualifications can be paralleled from other, similar, qualification lists elsewhere in the church order literature, namely *Didache* 15.1, *Apostolic Church Order* 16 and 18.2, *Didascalia of the Apostles* 2.1–2.6.1, and, fundamentally, 1 Timothy 3.1–13 with Titus 1.6–9, though no list is identical. Closest to that of the *Testament* is the *Didascalia* list. Beyond these lists in the church order literature we may also suggest that the reference to being in the place of God has literary history in Ignatius.[82] It is a list of qualifications that, moreover, suits the episcopal ministry as it was practised in these contexts, namely an economic ministry of support and leadership, administering the church's funds in support of the poor and

[80] See, in detail, my *Original Bishops* (Grand Rapids, MI: Baker Academic, 2014), 144–178, 268–294.

[81] *Testament* 1.20.

[82] Ignatius, *Magnesians* 6.1. Though it should be noted that the text is uncertain.

the widows. It does not, however, suit the bishop as his duties are prescribed within the *Testament*. In particular we may observe the provision that the bishop might be married, even though preference is expressed for a celibate (in exactly the terminology and phrasing of *Apostolic Church Order* 16.2). This does not fit with the ascetic who actually is the bishop.

The same observation, namely that the qualification list is traditional but not suited to the actual duties, may be made of the presbyteral qualification list at 1.29. The one point that may be observed with regard to this particular list is that, beyond the conventional economic expectations (he is to be as a father to orphans, and ministering to the poor) the presbyter here is also seen as the recipient of charismata.

All this indicates that the lists are not the composition of the redactor. Rather, existing qualification lists have been employed as part of the construction of the *Testament*, perhaps growing out of a hypothetical document whose existence I have proposed elsewhere, and termed the *Katastasis tou klērou* ("Appointment of clergy").[83] We can only speculate whether the inclusion of these lists was the work of a redactor, or whether they were already attached to the version of *Apostolic Tradition* circulating in this area. Nonetheless we may observe that this considerably complicates the matter of charting the history of the composition of the *Testament*.

By complete contrast we may note the qualification list for deacons at 1.33. This has little traditional material, and is entirely practical and suited to the ministry that the deacon is to exercise. He is not necessarily an ascetic (though he may be). This suggests that, rather than being derived from a source, it is, like the description of the deacons' duties, the work of the redactor.

[83] I argue for the existence of this lost church order in my *The Apostolic Church Order* (Strathfield NSW: St Paul's, 2006), 55–70. It is named after Harnack.

3.4.5: THE CHAPTER ON WILLS AND DEATH

The oddity about this chapter is not only that this interrupts the flow of the material regarding Pascha, which has already been disrupted by *Apostolic Tradition* material, and further disrupts this *Apostolic Tradition* material by coming in the middle of two chapters regarding the offering of firstfruits. Beyond that, one might have expected this material to be attached to the material on a similar topic derived from *Apostolic Tradition* at 2.23. This may be seen alongside the other oddity relating to the redactor's use of *Apostolic Tradition*, which lies in the displacement of *Apostolic Tradition* 36 and 38 (which is found in the middle of material from *Apostolic Tradition* 22—see the table below). One may suspect some accidental displacement of material at these points, though it is hard to determine precisely what.

Although this chapter may well reflect the realities of the congregational life of the *Testament* (in particular in providing for those who wish to take up the ascetic life), it is hard to assign it to a written source. The apparently freestanding appearance of this material may be the result of accidental displacement.

3.5: *Conclusion*

Having examined the material that is not derived from *Apostolic Tradition* (excluding the opening apocalypse and the mystagogy, and putting aside those parts that may have been dislocated), we may observe the following order:

- Instructions regarding church buildings
- Instructions regarding the bishop, including liturgical material
- Instructions regarding presbyters, including liturgical material
- Instructions regarding deacons, including liturgical material
- Instructions regarding widows, including liturgical material
- Miscellaneous instructions relating to Pascha

Although this has a logical order, it is also close to the order of *Apostolic Tradition* itself. As such we cannot be sure whether *Apostolic Tradition* has been interspersed with a distinct written source, or whether the additional material is from a variety of sources, some of which may have been oral. The very proximity of the order of the additional material to that of *Apostolic Tradition* might lead one to suspect that the source, or sources, were not an established written tradition but were in part at least committed to writing by virtue of the redactor's expansion of *Apostolic Tradition* to create the *Testament*. Some sources, however, were certainly written; the introductory apocalypse manifestly had independent literary existence, as did the mystagogy. It is also possible that the prayers of the people, the presbyters, and the widows may have had prior written existence. White points out that the widows' dawn prayer fits the context of an individual ascetic rather than one associated in some way with a church, and thus that the prayer has been adapted for inclusion in the *Testament*;[84] this implies a written source. We may also point to the paschal material and suggest that 2.12 and 2.18–20 read together make a coherent, if brief, account of Pascha, in spite of echoes of *Apostolic Tradition* in 2.20.

Other material, however, is highly likely to have been the product of the redactor. Thus we may point to the discussion of deacons' duties, which is clearly embedded in *Apostolic Tradition* material, and may be seen as offering a corrective and supplement to what the Hippolytean document had to say, in order that it might reflect the realities of the congregation known to the redactor.

It is difficult to be certain what is redactional and what is derived from a source, because the *Testament* redactor is certainly sympathetic to this earlier material, and derives from the same community that had produced it. Thus at 1.16, which is part of the apparatus of pseudonymy, the dialogue surrounding the appearance of Jesus and the springboard for the church order material, the women present, Martha, Mary, and Salome, ask regarding their duties and are told:

[84]White, *Daily Prayer*, 81.

"I desire that you should continue in intercession, that you should serve my gospel at all times, that you should show forth in yourselves a type of holiness for the salvation of those who patiently trust in me and that in all things you should be a likeness of the kingdom of the heavens." This describes the duties and life of the widows of the *Testament*. As such it would be hard to tell the free composition of the redactor apart from his sources. However, the probability is that the redactor has combined a number of written sources, and some orally transmitted material with which he was in sympathy, with *Apostolic Tradition*. The difficulty lies in identifying what was written and what was not, though this is of relatively minor significance since all derived from the same milieu.

We may, in this light, give brief consideration to White's suggestion. He tentatively identifies an earlier written source that he describes as a "hypothetical ascetic source" consisting of (a) a preface (1.1–3, 12–19a), (b) the dawn synaxis (1.2–28), (c) presbyters' ascetic rules (1.40–43), (d) widows' ascetic rules (the latter part of 2.11), and (e) a conclusion (2.26–27).[85]

I think that enough has been shown to sustain the suggestion that (b), (c), and (d), the central ascetic directions and prayer texts, belong together and might form a coherent mass. I think he is also correct in excluding the diaconal material; as I have already suggested, this is the work of a redactor who is supplementing and correcting *Apostolic Tradition*.

His identification of the preface, however, I find very uncertain, as much of this seems to be part of the apparatus of pseudonymy that would, in turn, be necessitated by the prefacing of the apocalypse, whether by the same redactor who combined material with *Apostolic Tradition* or by a further hand. I would suggest that the material in 1.17–18 would be sufficient to form such a preface. The same objection, namely that this is part of the apparatus of pseudonymy necessitated by the addition of the apocalypse, applies to White's identification of 2.26–27 as the conclusion. Part of 2.25,

[85]White, *Daily Prayer*, 158–159.

however, may supply such a conclusion. Most unlikely of all is the suggestion that 2.11, the *lucernarium*, formed part of this ascetic source; it is a derivation from *Apostolic Tradition*. It is, however, possible that the paschal material might have found a place in such an ascetic source. The duplication of provision for baptism at Pascha that would result from retaining 2.20, even after 2.8 had been supplied from *Apostolic Tradition*, is certainly an indication that we are dealing with a written source here, even if distinct from the main *askētikon*.

In summary, whereas we cannot be certain of the nature or extent of the sources which the redactor has combined with *Apostolic Tradition*, we may be assured that some of this additional material had an earlier existence prior to its inclusion in the *Testament*, that the redactor of the *Testament* had emerged from the community in which this earlier material had been generated, and that the redactor further supplied material from his own hand. Material produced by the redactor, nonetheless, reflects the practices and presuppositions of the community from which the document derived as much as any source that might have been employed, whether written or oral. As such, this material, layered into the Hippolytean substructure, provides clues to the origin of the document, in turn allowing the *Testament* to inform us further concerning the liturgy and theology of the community for which it was produced.

4: The Date and Provenance of the *Testament*

A bewildering variety of dates and provenances have been proposed for the *Testament*. Early treatments, such as that of Rahmani, tended to offer an early date for the *Testament*, though this preceded the realization that it was a derivation from *Apostolic Tradition*, then unrecognized, and so it was the primitive features in *Apostolic Tradition* rather than the material peculiar to the *Testament* which gave rise to the early dating. The standard line in encyclopedias is that the *Testament* is from the fourth (or fifth) century and from

Syria,[86] though how exactly this consensus emerged is hard to tell;[87] the repetition of such a statement simply bears witness to the lack of attention paid to this document for over a century. However, rather than reviewing opinions we might be better served observing what positively can be asserted about the *Testament* and proceeding from there.

4.1: Significant Characteristics of the Testament

4.1.1: ASCETICISM AND PRAYER

The *Testament* does not bear witness to organized cenobitic monasticism, but does point to ascetic practice centered on the local church. Thus the directions of *Apostolic Tradition* regarding the bishop are extended through a discussion of the fasting that is to be undertaken, and then of the daily prayer that the bishop is to undertake with the people.

Even more striking in this regard is the expansion of the Hippolytean material on the presbyterate. So much emphasis is placed on the prayer practice of the presbyter that White concludes that the presbyter in this circle has more of the older meaning of the term, an older man, than an ordained office. As such he sees the presbyter as more or less a male equivalent to the widows who have such prominence in the *Testament*.[88] Whereas it might be objected that the presbyter in the *Testament* is ordained, and is thus rather more than an older man, we may respond by suggesting that this is a confusion that has come about as this material is united with the *Apostolic Tradition*, a document whose agenda in part is to undermine the traditional presbyters. We may also observe that the word

[86]Authorities, largely dependent on the previous, are listed by Bruno Steimer, *Vertex traditionis: Die Gattung der altchristlichen Kirchenordnungen* (Berlin: de Gruyter, 1992), 100–101.

[87]It may have derived from F. X. Funk, *Das Testament des Herrn und die verwandten Schriften* (Mainz: Franz Kirchheim, 1901), who was convinced that the *Testament* was dependent on *Apostolic Constitutions* 8, and therefore must have been later.

[88]White, *Daily Prayer*, 92–94.

employed for the appointment of the presbyter, apart from those points derived from *Apostolic Tradition*, is the same as that used for widows, and simply means "appoint" rather than "ordain." We have already noted, with White, the absence of any liturgical duty for the presbyter, agreeing with him that the presbyter's fundamental role, like that of the widow, is prayer and the practice of asceticism, and that even those teaching duties assigned to the presbyter are the guidance of ascetics, rather than catechesis and instruction of Christians more generally.[89]

It is most important, however, to note the manner in which this ascetic practice is seen as part of the life of a local church. In particular the deacons have responsibility for the distribution of the church's offerings, which may, we suggest, include support of the ascetics. As such we can see this as in keeping with the seventh canon of Gangra, which is clear that ascetics are not to help themselves to the offerings of the church, and which overall seems to envisage any ascetics as part of the localized Christian community.

4.1.2: THE PRAYER ADDRESSES TO THE FATHER AND TO THE SON

The prayer texts do not discriminate in their address to the Father and the Son, but career back and forth between the two. Thus, for instance, the exorcism prior to baptism (2.7) is addressed first to the "God of heaven," who is subsequently described as "Father of our Lord Jesus Christ." Then there is an address to the "Son and Word of God." After a number of attributes and recounting of the deeds of Christ, we hear, "Hear me, Lord, as I cry out to you in grief and fear." Although it is not clear to whom this address is made, this is soon clarified by what follows: "Lord God, Father of our Lord Jesus Christ. . . ." Similarly the nocturnal prayer of widows begins with an address to the God of Abraham and after a while is abruptly addressed to the "Son and Word and thought of the Father, Christ." These are not isolated incidents, as the phenomenon may be

[89]White, *Daily Prayer*, 92–98, 111–113.

observed throughout the material peculiar to the *Testament*. There is, however, no direct address to the Holy Spirit.[90]

Whereas this may be described as anti-Arian, it may better be characterized as simply "non-Arian." It reflects a conventional Asian Christology, found, for instance, in Melito of Sardis and the reported belief of Noetus from Smyrna.[91] Notably, this phenomenon is found in prayer texts and so does not reflect a considered theology as much as the wellspring of devotion.

However, in the baptismal interrogation, fundamentally derived from *Apostolic Tradition*, the *Testament*, uniquely among the witnesses to *Apostolic Tradition*, adds to the beginning of the second question (the additional phrase is italicized):

> Do you also believe in Christ Jesus the Son of God, *who is of the Father, who from the beginning was with the Father,* who was born from the Virgin Mary by the Holy Spirit . . .

This, reflecting the statement of the creed of Nicaea (though not that of Constantinople) that Christ was begotten of the *ousia* of the Father, may more certainly be described as anti-Arian. Whereas this is seen as Apollinarian by Wordsworth,[92] who notes the similarity of this phrasing to some points of the "detailed creed" attributed to Apollinarius,[93] we may again suggest that this is an anti-Arian response, held in common with Apollinarius. For all that Wordsworth finds echoes of Apollinarius here and in certain phrases from the mystagogy, as Cooper and McLean respond, there

[90]Though see the discussion of the so-called *epiklēsis* in the appendix below.

[91]Thus at *On Pascha* 9 Melito states that Christ "is Father, in that he begets. He is Son, in that he is begotten" and at *Against Noetus* 1.2 Noetus is reported as stating that "Christ was the Father, and that the Father had himself been begotten, suffered and died."

[92]J. Wordsworth, "The 'Testament of our Lord.' Part II: Its Connexion with the School of Apollinarius of Laodicea," *Church Quarterly Review* 99 (1900): 1–29.

[93]This credal statement may be found (in Greek and English) in Wolfram Kinzig, *Faith in Formulae: A Collection of Early Christian Creeds and Creed-Related Texts*, vol. 1 (Oxford: Oxford University Press, 2017), 438–443.

is nothing typically or uniquely Apollinarian in any of the statements of the *Testament*.[94]

Such a development reflects the manner in which those of a traditional Asian Christology might react to the Nicene debate. We may see the *Testament* therefore as alive to the controversies of the fourth century, but deriving from a similar theological tradition as that of Marcellus of Ancyra, without intending to focus on the specifics of the debate. For the redactor of the *Testament*, as for the tradition to which he was heir, Christ represented the Father, and the Father is known through Christ.

4.1.3: THE PROPHETIC ELEMENT IN THE *TESTAMENT*

In spite of the absence of any address to the Holy Spirit, the *Testament* shows a lively interest in the prophetic work of the Holy Spirit. Thus at 1.23 it is stated that those with spiritual gifts are to receive communion first after the clergy, at 1.32 there is reference to prophetic utterances in the context of daily prayer, at the election of widows (1.40) provision is made for the possibility that somebody has had a revelation regarding the candidate, and at 2.1 the bishop exhorts the candidate for baptism with prophetic statements. Such observations provided Rahmani with evidence that the *Testament* was a product of the second century[95] and led Morin to suggest that the *Testament* either was a Montanist work, or incorporated one.[96] In responding we should be careful in stating that a lively prophetic culture, whilst known within the Montanist circles of the second century on, was not restricted to these circles, or, within the majority church, to this period. Thus we may particularly note *Apostolic Church Order* 21, which legislates for two widows within the church who are to have revelations. Draper similarly points out that the Ethiopic transmission of the *Didache* may relate to Asian missionary activity in the fourth century, evidence that there was a

[94]Cooper and Maclean, *Testament,* 19–20.
[95]Rahmani, *Testamentum*, xlvii–xlviii.
[96]G. Morin, "Le Testament du Seigneur," *Revue Bénédictine* 17 (1900): 10–28.

continuing recognition of prophetic activity in Asian catholic circles in this period.[97] Montanist prophecy grew out of Asian Christianity, which had known the daughters of Philip,[98] Quadratus, Ammia, and others[99] functioning as prophets, and so we may anticipate "catholic" communities continuing to recognize prophetic practice. This is the situation of the *Testament*.

4.2: Further Considerations

The significant characteristics of the *Testament* that we discussed above indicate a context in the latter part of the fourth century, and most likely in Asia. In this light we may observe certain provisions of the Council of Laodicea. These canons seem to be operating in the same area of concern, even when they forbid practices found in the *Testament*, as these prohibitions indicate that these are practices known alike to each setting. Thus canon 11 forbids the appointment of female presbyters, older women whose role is akin to that of the widows of the *Testament*, canon 15 restricts those who may sing in church to those who sing out of a book from the ambo, to which we may contrast the provisions for hymnody in the *Testament* and canons 22 and 23, which indicate that the *orarion* is becoming a mark of ordination rather than a badge of office, whereas in the *Testament* this is the badge of the senior deacon.

We may also return to the *Apostolic Church Order*. This church order legislates against the liturgical involvement of women; I have already suggested that the provisions of the *Testament of the Lord*, or a similar community, have occasioned the church order's concern, and may reiterate that point here, with the further observation that *Apostolic Church Order* is probably Cappadocian in origin. All of this

[97]Jonathan Draper, "Performing the Cosmic Mystery of the Church in the Communities of the *Didache*," in *The Open Mind: Essays in Honour of Christopher Rowland, ed.* Jonathan Knight and Kevin Sullivan (London: Bloomsbury, 2015), 37–57, at 45–46.

[98]Eusebius, *Ecclesiastical History* 3.31.3–5.

[99]Eusebius, *Ecclesiastical History* 5.17.

points to a setting for the *Testament* to the east of Asia, which is to say Phrygia or Cappadocia, in the fourth century.

In this light we may observe the following (Phrygian) inscription from the fourth century:

> [Here lies] a prophetess: Nanas daughter of Hermogenes. With prayers and intercessions [she besought?] the praiseworthy master; | with hymns and adulations she implored the immortal one; praying all day and night long she possessedthe fear of God from the beginning. | Angelic visitations and speech she had in greatest measure: Nanas, the blessed one, whose "sleeping-place" . . . a | "sleeping-companion," a much-loved husband, has gone together with [her] . . . into the all-nourishing earth, a matter [calling for a sad] mind . . . he [she?], in turn, prepared . . . | Those who long after her have honored her greatly . . . (erecting this stele) as a memorial.[100]

There is debate as to whether Nanas is a Montanist or, as I suspect, a catholic Christian.[101] To an extent this does not matter. As a widow, as a prophet, as one who enjoyed the company of angels, and most importantly as somebody who would pray through the day and through the night, this Phrygian Christian from the fourth century represents to us a devotee to whom the practices of the *Testament of the Lord* would be familiar and fleshes out the picture drawn by the *Testament* of a group of ascetics joined to the church.

[100]Given here following William Tabbernee, *Montanist Inscriptions and Testimonia: Epigraphic Sources Illustrating the History of Montanism* (Macon, GA: Mercer University Press, 1997), 421. However, the phrase "angelic visitations and speech she had in greatest measure" may mean "she had angelic visitations and speech from the most-high ones."

[101]See Christine Trevett, "'Angelic Visitations and Speech She Had': Nanas of Kotiaeion," in *Prayer and Spirituality in the Early Church*, vol. 2, ed. Pauline Allen et al. (Brisbane: Centre for Early Christian Studies, 1999), 259–277 (Nanas as catholic), John C. Poirier, "The Montanist Nature of the Nanas Inscription (Steinepigramme 16/41/15)," *Epigraphica Anatolica* 37 (2004): 151–159; Vera Hirschmann, "'Nach Art der Engel': die phrygische Prophetin Nanas," *Epigraphica Anatolica* 37 (2004): 160–168 (Nanas as Montanist).

4.3: *Conclusion*

To locate the *Testament* in Cappadocia or in neighboring regions in the fourth century is hardly new. It was the suggestion of Cooper,[102] and has recently been revived by White.[103] We may claim, however, to have reinforced the old arguments with new ones. To summarize:

- The apocalypse, while of earlier origin, might well be appropriately recycled in Cappadocia or in nearby regions in the light of the Hunnic invasions of 395.
- The liturgical provisions, insofar as they can be reconstructed, particularly the baptismal rituals, are recognizable as those of the late fourth century; the baptismal rituals in particular can be readily compared to others of west Syrian and Asian provenance.
- The ascetic life described and the patterns of prayer are strikingly similar to the Basilian rules and the Pseudo-Athanasian and Cappadocian *On Virginity.*
- The theological presuppositions of the *Testament* with regard to Christology are those of a conservative Asian school.
- The provisions for senior widows seem to be those legislated at the Council of Laodicea.
- There is evidence of a Quartodeciman background in the provisions for Pascha and in the Asianist rhetoric of the paschal proclamation (here described as a mystagogy).
- The prophetic elements within the *Testament* are entirely at home in a fourth-century Cappadocian setting.
- The pre-history of office in this community, insofar as it can be reconstructed, is that of an episcopal-diaconal system,

[102]Cooper and Maclean, *Testament*, 41–45.
[103]White, *Daily Prayer*, 160–162.

> with presbyters as a distinct group. While this group is, in the *Testament,* ascetic, rather than patronal, this reflects a development of the traditional Asian system.

The only other recent treatment of the *Testament* is that of Kohlbacher, who attempts to locate this production in anti-Chalcedonian circles in Palestine in the latter part of the fifth century.[104] This can hardly work: not only is there no reference in the *Testament* to Lent, in spite of discussing periods of fasting and baptismal preparation, or Christmas, in spite of the mention of a festal calendar, but the complete absence of any reference to organized monasticism, and the expectation that the ascetic focus is in the local church, is entirely foreign to the climate of fifth-century Palestine.

It is likely that the bulk of the material was put into literary form in the course of the fourth century, and then prefaced with the apocalypse towards the end of that century. Given that the bulk of the material points to a fourth-century origin in Asia, and given that this material is worked closely into the material derived from *Apostolic Tradition*, and prefaced with an older apocalypse that would have chilling echoes at the end of the fourth century, this period and provenance are also most likely to be considered the principal date and location of redaction likewise.

Seeing the *Testament* as the product of fourth-century Cappadocia, we may advance a highly provisional compositional history for the document.

At the heart lies an ascetic manual, for the direction of the life of prayer of a bishop, with a cadre of ascetics, male (presbyters) and female (widows). The people are to participate on occasion in this prayer, particularly in the concluding vigil on Sabbath and Sunday mornings before the celebration of the Eucharist, and at Pascha.

[104]Michael Kohlbacher, "Wessen Kirche ordnete das *Testamentum Domini Nostri Jesu Christi?* Anmerkungen zum historischen Kontext von CPG 1743," in *Zu Geschichte, Theologie, Liturgie und Gegenwartslage der syrischen Kirchen*, ed. Martin Tamcke and Andreas Heinz (Münster: Lit, 2000), 55–137.

This manual was combined with *Apostolic Tradition* at some point in the fourth century.

An older qualification list is also present, though we cannot know whether it was incorporated at the same time as the combination with *Apostolic Tradition*, or had already become attached to *Apostolic Tradition*. It was not part of the ascetic manual, due to the contradictions between this qualification list and the ascetic requirements of the bishop and presbyters.

Other material, certainly the description of deacons' duties, probably the material about death and wills (2.15), and possibly the description of church buildings, was the composition of the redactor, undertaken at the time of combination.

Either this work of composition was completed in the later fourth century with the further combination of a pre-existent apocalypse, or else the composition was made earlier in the fourth century, and then supplemented with the apocalypse and other pseudonymous material, at the end of the fourth century. To an extent this uncertainty is insignificant; what is significant is identifying the sources and the redactional composition, and assigning to them a date and provenance in fourth-century Cappadocia.

5: General Conclusion

In the opening of this introduction it was observed that the *Testament of the Lord* is conventionally classified as a church order even as some allusion was made to the debate over the legitimacy of this term. A further issue for debate is the extent to which these church orders were normative, and to what extent they present idealized accounts of worship.

The *Testament* presents composite rites in which native material is joined to a distinct liturgical tradition derived from *Apostolic Tradition*. It is not impossible that composite rites were practiced (there are many Anglican baptismal rites with two professions of faith!). However, the *Testament*, I suggest, in its extant form, is not the description of a real church and its liturgy. It is an artificial construction, of conservative hue, the sense of artificiality being brought about through the combination of material from third-century Rome with local material.

The reason for the redactor's procedure in incorporating *Apostolic Tradition* is hard to see, though it is possible that it represented an attempt to combine the ascetic handbook with a more normal liturgical order, in pursuit of the redactor's vision of asceticism at the heart of the local church. We may note the presence of Messalianism in this area at the proposed time of the redaction of the *Testament*. The Messalians believed that perfection, freedom from the passions and thus release from the earthly realm, is attained by prayer alone, and so denied the efficacy of baptism, and sacraments, thus effectively denying any function to the Church. We may therefore, rather speculatively, suggest that incorporating a church order with a detailed rite of baptism and extensive exorcisms into the ascetic handbook would protect the circle employing the handbook from any suggestion of Messalian sympathies, for if the *Testament* community's emphasis on prayer and the search for perfection might lead to suspicion, then publicly to assert the manner of celebrating sacraments in this ascetic community would deflect suspicion.

The rationale behind the combination of this order with the opening apocalypse, however, is easier to discern, as the prefaced apocalypse adds a context for the *Testament's* call to holiness. The Jesus of the apocalypse instructs that "those who fear my words and who perform them in truth with a faithful mind shall keep watch and pray without ceasing, reckoning it their duty to offer prayers at all times."[105] The Testament provides the texts by which and the context in which this may be done.

Although the *Testament* is a construct, the community for which it was written was a real community, and the material with which *Apostolic Tradition* was combined was real material in the use of that community. Thus, in particular, the long stretches of material in the

[105] *Testament* 1.13.

Testament concerning the duties of presbyters and the widows, and their prayer, represent the practice of this Christian community, and I believe that I have further shown that removal of *Apostolic Tradition* material from other rites can expose still more of the practice of this community. The juncture of this material in turn with the apocalypse with which the work opens (itself pre-existent material) was undertaken as a call to the Church to maintain sanctity in its life, and the order as a whole encourages the close involvement of ascetics in the life of the local church, as opposed to their separation in monastic communities.

As such, the *Testament*, for all its artificiality, perhaps still has something to teach us.

EXCURSUS

The "Epiclesis"

Particular issues pertain to the *Testament*'s handling of the so-called epiclesis of *Apostolic Tradition*. Before turning to the justification of the translation offered here we should discuss the history of interpretation.

The initial translation by Rahmani, following the Mosul MS, read as follows: "To you do we offer this thanksgiving, eternal Trinity, O Lord Jesus Christ, O Lord the Father, O Lord the Holy Spirit . . . Bring this drink and this food of your holiness, and cause that they may be for us. . . ."[1] The verb is *ʾtʾ*, which means "to come." Here it is in what is called the aphel (causative), which may thus mean "bring," and Rahmani understands it in this sense. The form he understands as a feminine singular imperative (*ʾtʾy*), which he takes as addressed to the Trinity.[2]

For Cooper and Maclean "this scarcely makes sense." Thus, rather than beginning the request with "bring," they adopt a reading from the Borgian Syriac MS, *ʾtʾyn*, a participle, rather than the imperative *ʾtʾy* of the Mosul MS, and translate: "We have brought this drink and this food of thy Holiness to thee. Cause that it may be to us. . . ."[3] They find support for this in one Ethiopic version of the anaphora of the *Testament*, published by Ludolf.[4] The problem with this solution is that the Borgian Syriac text is generally poor.

[1] Here translating from Rahmani's Latin.

[2] Rahmani, *Testamentum*, 188–189 clarifies this point.

[3] Cooper and Maclean, *Testament*, 74.

[4] This is the so-called "Anaphora of Our Lord" published by Ludolf in 1691, and given in English by Cooper and Maclean, *Testament*, in an appendix, 245–248. There is no modern edition.

Although Dix and Richardson commented briefly on this passage,[5] in the context of an argument over the epiclesis of *Apostolic Tradition*, the next major contribution to the debate was that of Botte,[6] responding to Richardson's brief comment. In particular Botte suggests that the verb *ʾtʾy* in the aphel might equally well be a rendition of "send." This is possible. As a feminine imperative he suggests it is addressed to the Spirit, but that the Syriac translator had failed to understand that in the Greek the word was accusative (the form would be the same in Greek) and that the petition to "send" was not originally addressed to the Spirit but to the Father, and that the Spirit was the object. Thus the original would have read: "Lord, send the Holy Spirit on this holy drink and this food. . . ."

One merit of Botte's suggestion is that an object is supplied; something, it seems, needs to come, or be sent, onto the gifts so that they may not be for condemnation, and the object is not the food and drink. Thus while it is tempting to accept Cooper and Maclean's adoption of the reading of B and so to make this passage a continuation of the oblation, making the food and drink the objects means that no account is taken of the word *l* ("to" or "onto") which precedes these words.

Richardson, in response, found Botte's suggestions entirely unconvincing. If the Syriac translator had so misunderstood the Greek accusative, he argues, then this would mean that he had completely missed the address to the Trinity, and the threefold "Lord" that it contains. Thus the Spirit cannot be an object, but is simply addressed as part of the Trinity. In seeking an object he turns his attention to the Syriac *d* which is attached to the word translated "holiness", and suggests that this represents a partitive genitive. Thus he translates: "Send (O Trinity) a portion of thy Holiness on this drink and food.

[5]Gregory Dix, *The Treatise on the Apostolic Tradition of St Hippolytus of Rome* (London: SPCK, 1937), 75–79; C.C. Richardson, "The So-called Epiclesis in Hippolytus," *Harvard Theological Review* 40 (1947): 101–108.

[6]Bernard Botte, "L'epiclèse de l'anaphore d'Hippolyte," *Recherches de Théologie Ancienne et Médiévale* 14 (1947): 241–251.

Cause that it may be to us...."[7] Bouyer similarly wonders whether the Syriac text is so obscure as to oblige us to have recourse to the suggestion of such a series of errors on the part of the Syriac translator, though in effect his suggestions return us to Rahmani's reading.[8]

White's translation is interesting. He seems to accept the reading of B, with Cooper and Maclean, but unlike them takes the whole phrase as addressed to the Holy Spirit: "Lord Holy Spirit, we have brought this food and drink of your holiness; make it be for us...."[9] It seems odd to find an oblation to the Holy Spirit, but it is significant that he can see that the phrase might be addressed to the Spirit. This accounts for the feminine form of the imperative. It seems that he has accepted Botte's suggestion that the translator had mistaken an accusative for a vocative, but unlike Botte translates the Syriac text as it stands, taking the feminine imperative as addressed to the (feminine) Spirit rather than correcting it (as Botte does) in accordance with a hypothetical Greek original.

More recent treatments have not advanced the debate. McKenna simply agrees with Botte without any discussion of the Syriac text,[10] and McGowan likewise pays no mind to the Syriac text, or to any possible underlying Greek, offering us the following translation (in which the debt to Botte is evident), which she has derived from elsewhere:

> We offer to you this act of thanksgiving, eternal Trinity, Lord Jesus Christ, Lord Father, from whom all creation and all nature trembles as it flees into itself, Lord, send your Holy Spirit upon this drink and upon this your holy food. Grant that it may not be for us condemnation.... [11]

[7]"A Note on the Epicleses in Hippolytus and the Testamentum Domini," *Recherches de Théologie Ancienne et Médiévale* 15 (1948): 357–359.

[8]Bouyer, *Eucharist*, 171–175.

[9]Grant (Sperry-)White, *The Testamentum Domini: A Text for Students* (Bramcote: Grove, 1991), 17.

[10]John H. McKenna, *The Eucharistic Epiclesis: A Detailed History*, 2nd ed. (Chicago, IL: Hillenbrand, 2009), 9–11.

[11]Anne McGowan, *Eucharistic Epicleses Ancient and Modern* (London: SPCK, 2014), 81–82. This has a chilling similarity to the Latin translation offered by A. Raes

Before discussing the possibilities presented, the one contribution that I may make is to observe that the Arabic edited by Troupeau clearly understands that the Trinity is addressed. The Trinity is bidden: "make that this holy food and this drink of sanctification may not be condemnation for us . . ."[12] thus missing out the verb in dispute. The imperative is masculine.

The question may perhaps be reopened in the light of our observation that the prayer as it stands is the result of combining two anaphoras.

We may recollect that Botte's suggestion was criticized by Richardson on the basis of the violence it did to the address to the Trinity. However, it is possible that, in keeping with other prayers in the *Testament*, the Trinity as such was not addressed, but rather only the Father and the Son. This would explain the odd order found here, with the Son first. Thus the original, prior to the combination with *Apostolic Tradition*, might have read:

> To you do we offer this thanksgiving, eternal Trinity, O Lord Jesus Christ, O Lord the Father, from whom every creature and every nature escapes into itself in trembling; send some of your holiness onto this drink and this food. . . .

The text of *Apostolic Tradition* facing the redactor is itself an uncertain matter, but it is highly probable that it read (as Botte suggested), "we ask that you should send your Holy Spirit. . . ." As such it is possible that the mention of the Holy Spirit should be taken from *Apostolic Tradition*, and the words "Holy Spirit" supplied from that source. However much it may seem that the three persons of the Trinity are addressed in the *Testament*, this is the result of the juncture of two sources.

The Holy Spirit in *Apostolic Tradition* was the object. However, given the redactor's freedom with the source, faced with the necessity

in *Prex eucharistica*, ed. Anton Hänggi, Irmgard Pahl (Fribourg: Éditions Universitaires, 1968), 221.

[12]Troupeau, "Version Arabe," 251.

of combining two prayers, and given that the sentence already had an object (the portion of holiness), I suggest that he deliberately turned this into a vocative, and thus addresses the Holy Spirit directly at this point. There are thus two addresses, one to the Father and the Son, and one to the Holy Spirit. The rightness of White's translation at this point becomes manifest when it is observed that this mention of the Spirit supplied from *Apostolic Tradition* has been inserted into an existing prayer. As such the change of case that results is also less significant than Richardson thought. He suggests, against Botte, that it is improbable that the translator would so misunderstand the original as to read an accusative as a vocative; the suggestion here is that there was no misreading, and that this is not the work of a later translator, but that the translator accurately rendered a deliberate change that had already been made by the redactor.

The result is thus a combination of the insights of Botte, who reconstructs the original of *Apostolic Tradition,* Richardson, who supplies an object by reading *d* in the Syriac text as representing a partitive genitive, and White, who so punctuates that such that the address to the Spirit stands out, all understood through the lens of the redactor's layering technique. The address is directed to the Holy Spirit (the mention of whom is supplied from *Apostolic Tradition*), the object is taken as "a portion of holiness," and the address to the Trinity recognized as an accident of redaction.

As a result of this I have translated: "To you do we offer this thanksgiving, eternal Trinity, O Lord Jesus Christ, O Lord the Father, from whom every creature and every nature escapes into itself in trembling. O Lord, Holy Spirit, send some of your holiness onto this drink and this food. . . ."

Table: The Correspondence between
Apostolic Tradition and *The Testament of the Lord*

Testament of the Lord	*Apostolic Tradition*
1.1–20	Not paralleled
Not paralleled	1
1.21	2–3
1.22	Not paralleled
1.23	4
1.24–25	5–6 (though material substituted in entirety)
1.26–29	Not paralleled
1.30	7
1.31–1.37	Not paralleled
1.38–41	8–10 (though 10 is greatly expanded)
1.42–43	Not paralleled
1.44–47	11–14
2.1–10	15–22, 38 (The material from chapter 38 is incorporated within that derived from chapter 22.)
	23 (Not paralleled, but this duplicates material elsewhere.)
2.11	24–25
2.12	Not paralleled
2.13–14	26–31 (13 substantially abbreviates and rewrites *Apostolic Tradition* 26–30)
2.15	Not paralleled
2.16	32
2.17	Not paralleled
2.18–21	33–34 (18–20 substantially alters and expands *Apostolic Tradition* 33)
2.22	Not paralleled
	35 This chapter is a doublet of part of *Apostolic Tradition* 41. There were two extant conclusions to *Apostolic Tradition*, and the redactor of the *Testament* was in possession of one that did not include this chapter. It is not, therefore, a deliberate omission on the part of the redactor.
	37, 39

	(38, see 22 above.)
2.23	40
2.24	41
	42 (Not paralleled, but this duplicates material elsewhere.)
2.25	36, 43
2.26–27	Not paralleled

The Testament of the Lord

ENGLISH VERSION

In the notes:

Ethiopic refers to Roger Beylot, *Testamentum Domini éthiopien: Édition et traduction* (Leuven: Peeters, 1984).

Rahmani's text refers to the Syriac text published by Ignatius Ephraem II Rahmani, *Testamentum Domini nostri Jesu Christi* (Mainz: Kirchheim, 1899) based on a manuscript in the patriarchal library at Mosul.

The Borgian Arabic refers to the MS Borg. Ar. 22, known entirely through Rahmani's references to it in his notes.

The Borgian Syriac refers to the MS Borg. Syr. 148.

The Cambridge-Paris fragment refers to the apocalyptic text edited independently by J. P. Arendzen, "A New Syriac Text of the Apocalyptic Part of the 'Testament of the Lord,'" *Journal of Theological Studies* 2 (1901): 401–416 and F. Nau, "Fragment inedit d'une traduction syriaque jusqu'ici inconnue du Testamentum D.N. Jesu Christi," *Journal Asiatique* 17 (1901): 233–256.

The Greek witness in the notes to 2.7 refers to the prayers from medieval Greek euchologia published by B. Gain, "Fragments grecs inédits du Testamentum Domini attribués à Saint Basile," *Augustinianum* 32 (1992): 261–277.

The Paris manuscript refers to Paris BN Syr. 62 (formerly known as Codex Sangermanensis 38) published by P. de Lagarde, *Reliquiae* *iuris ecclesiastici antiquissimae, graece et syriace* (Leipzig: Teubner, 1856), 2–19.

The Synodicon text refers to the portions of the *Testament* found in the west Syrian *Synodicon* (Arthur Vööbus, ed., *The Synodicon in the West Syrian Tradition*, 2 vols. in 4 pts., Corpus Scriptorum Christianorum Orientalium 367–368 and 375–376 [Leuven: Peeters, 1975/76]).

1

The Testament, otherwise the words which our Lord spoke to the holy apostles after he rose from the dead, and which were written by Clement of Rome, the disciple of Peter, in eight books[1]

It happened that after our Lord rose from the dead he appeared to us, and was touched by Thomas and Matthew and John.[2] We were utterly convinced that our teacher had truly risen from the dead. Then we fell on our faces, blessing God, the Father of a new world[3] who saved us through Jesus Christ our Lord. So much were we struck down[4] with fear that we remained prostrate like infants. But then our Lord Jesus laid a hand on all of us, one by one. He stood us up and said: "Why are you so downcast in your hearts and why struck down with such astonishment? Do you not know that the one who sent me can do great things for the salvation of those who believe in him in their hearts? So do not stand stunned, as if you were seeing things, and do not be negligent, but as children of the light ask for the spirit of counsel and might[5] from my Father in heaven.

[1]Title according to Rahmani's text and the Synodicon. This is, of course, the title to the entire Octateuch.

[2]Cf. Jn 20.27; 1 Jn 1.1.

[3]The Paris MS has "Father of the world."

[4]The Paris MS has "trembled." The roots are very similar in this form.

[5]Cf. Is 11.2.

And he will fill you with the Holy Spirit. As he gives it to you, so you will be with me forever."

1 We made answer to him as we said: "Lord, what is the Holy Spirit that you say we should request, and what is his power?"[6] Our Lord said to us: "Truly do I say to you, you shall not be sons of light except by means of the Holy Spirit." We made answer to him as we said: "Lord, give us this." Straightaway Jesus breathed on us.[7] And after we had received the Holy Spirit he said to us: "Truly do I say to you, that you who are become disciples of the kingdom of heaven, who have put your faith in me with no doubt in your heart, who are joined to me, shall be with me. And all those who, through you, know and do the will of my Father, who keep my words and know of my sufferings, shall be sanctified and shall abide in my Father's dwellings and shall be safe from the evil days that are coming. And I shall be with them and shall show them my ways, by which they may live."

2 Peter and John answered him and said: "Lord, tell us the signs of the end[8] and all that shall be done at that time by those[9] who are living in this world, so that we may make them known to all who believe in your name from all the nations, so that those generations may keep them and live." Jesus, however, answered and said: "Before I suffered for those who dwell upon the earth, when I was speaking with you, did I not tell you something beforehand about the end?" We made answer and said: "Lord, but now we wish to know the occurrences that are the signs of the destruction of this world, if our Lord should consider it fitting, both for us and for those who are to hear."

[6]So Rahmani's text. The Ethiopic adds: "of which you say 'Request it of my Father.'"

[7]Cf. Jn 20.22.

[8]Mk 13.3–4.

[9]Here following the Cambridge-Paris fragment, rather than Rahmani's text.

3 Jesus answered and said: "In my own time,[10] before I was glorified, I spoke to you of the signs that would show that the end was approaching. There would be famines and plagues on the earth, disorder and commotion as nations rise up against nations, and everything else of which I spoke to you. However, I commanded you to be watchful and prayerful. Listen then, you who are sons of light. Since my Father, who sent me to his inheritance, determined in advance, in his foreknowledge, that there should be vessels, hallowed and honorable and chosen, in the last days from the final generations, so I make known to you exactly what shall happen, and when the son of perdition, the enemy, the adversary, shall arise and what he is like."

4 "These shall be the signs when the kingdom is coming near: After the famines and plagues and disorders among the nations, then princes who love money shall rule and come to power, who are enemies of the truth, who kill their brothers, liars, who hate the faithful, who are proud, who love gold. Then there shall be kings reigning in the east, who are inglorious, thoughtless, immature, boys who love gold,[11] of a single race but not of a single mind, as each seeks to destroy the life of their allies. However, within their forces there shall be great disturbance, and flight, and bloodshed."

5 "There shall arise in the west another gentile King, a leader of great cunning, godless, a murderer, a deceiver, a lover of gold, extremely devious, wicked, a hater of the faithful and a persecutor.[12] He shall hold sway over the nations of the barbarians and shall shed much

[10]The reading of the Paris MS. Others have "At the time of my persecution" and "at the time when I was in the world." Any of these are plausible.

[11]The first part of this sentence is entirely supplied from the Cambridge-Paris fragment. It is certain that it was omitted in the other manuscripts due to the double appearance of "who love gold."

[12]Cf. the Cambridge-Paris fragment: "of great cunning, godless, a murderer, a deceiver, mighty, with many plans, scheming, a hater of the faith, a boaster, a persecutor of the Christians."

blood. Then silver shall be despised and gold honoured; in every city and in every land there shall be despoliation and robbery and bloodshed."

6 "Then shall there be signs in the heaven. A bow shall be seen in the heavens,[13] and a horn, and lights, untimely sounds and voices,[14] and raging in the sea and a roaring of the earth."

7 "Moreover there shall be signs on the earth. Dragons shall be born of people, and the same will occur to the wild animals. Young girls just married to their husbands[15] will give birth to babies who speak perfectly,[16] announcing the last days and pleading to be killed. They shall have the appearance of men of advanced years as they will be white-haired[17] when they are born. But women shall give birth to babies with four legs. Others shall give birth to spirits alone, whereas others shall give birth with unclean spirits. Others shall practice divination in the womb, conversing with the spirits of the dead,[18] and there shall be many other horrible signs."[19]

8 "There will be great disorder among assemblies[20] and churches and nations, for wicked shepherds shall arise who are unjust,

[13]"In the heavens" is supplied following the Cambridge-Paris fragment and the Latin. It is not in the other Syriac MSS.

[14]For "untimely sounds and voices" the Cambridge-Paris fragment reads "untimely thunders and lightnings and a sound of all kinds of storms."

[15]Rahmani's text. The Cambridge-Paris fragment refers to young men just married. Arendzen, "New Syriac Text," 407n2, suggests that the translator took the Greek *neogamoi* as a masculine.

[16]Cf. 2 Esd 6.21.

[17]"White-haired," in the Ethiopic. Latin and Rahmani's text have "white" whereas the Cambridge-Paris fragment has "old men." I suggest that "white-haired" stood in Jacob's translation, since the phrase is employed to describe a venerable man, and so the text might be corrupted through losing the term "haired." Ethiopic has preserved this. Cf. Jubilees 23.25: "and the heads of the children will be white, with grey hair" and Cyprian *To Demetrian* 4.1, who refers to children with white hair as a sign of the ageing of the world and the approach of the end.

[18]The Cambridge-Paris fragment omits this phrase.

[19]On these unnatural births cf. 2 Esd 5.8.

[20]The Cambridge-Paris fragment and the Latin omit the mention of assemblies.

negligent, greedy. Lovers of luxury, lovers of gain, garrulous, boastful, proud, gluttonous,[21] perverted, senseless, licentious, vainglorious, who go in a way opposed to the gospel, far distant from the narrow gateway,[22] who distance themselves from suffering and have no thought for my passion. They despise all words of truth, scorning every way of piety; they have no sorrow for their sins. And so shall disbelief spread among the nations, hatred of brothers, wickedness, bitterness, contempt, envy, hatred, contention, theft, greed, drunkenness, gluttony, lasciviousness, licentiousness, fornication, and all deeds which are opposed to the commandments of life. The majority shall avoid sorrow and humility, peace and gentleness, and poverty and pity and mourning as the shepherds heard[23] of such deeds but did not do them. Indeed they did not teach my commandments, as they were themselves examples of wickedness in the nation. The time shall come when some of them will deny me, and will bring about tumult upon the earth and shall put their trust in corruptible kings.[24] Yet those who put their trust in my name shall live at the last."[25]

"Then they shall establish commandments for people unlike the book of the commandments that are in accordance with my Father's will.[26] Those who are chosen[27] and sanctified to me shall be despised by them, and shall be called polluted by them. It is they, however, who are upright, pure, contrite, merciful, gentle, kind, who know at all times who it is who is among them forever. They shall be called

[21]This word is supplied from the Cambridge-Paris fragment supported by the Paris MS.

[22]Cf. Mt 7.13.

[23]"Heard," so the Cambridge-Paris fragment, supported by the Paris MS. Rahmani's text has "hated."

[24]The plural is read in keeping with the Cambridge-Paris fragment, the Paris MS, and the Synodicon text. Rahmani's text has a singular.

[25]Mt 10.22, 24.13; Mk 13.13.

[26]Cf. the Cambridge-Paris fragment, which reads: "commandments not according to my will and and traditions that are not in accordance with my Father's will."

[27]"Chosen" is taken from the Cambridge-Paris fragment, supported by the Paris MS. Rahmani's text simply has "men."

mad on account of me, the one who has redeemed[28] them. In those days my Father will gather together the just ones of that generation, those who are pure and faithful. To them shall I appear and make my dwelling among them. And I shall send to them an understanding of knowledge and truth, and an understanding of holiness. And they shall not cease from praising and giving thanks to their God, the Father who sent me. At all times shall they speak the truth and shall instruct those whose spirit they test and find upright and worthy of the kingdom, and shall teach them in knowledge and fortitude and understanding. And those who are persecuted because they live piously shall obtain the reward of their praiseworthy deeds."

"In those times every kingdom shall be disturbed and the whole world shall undergo affliction and want. This whole world shall be reckoned as nothing, and all its goods shall be destroyed by many (destroyers). The scarcity of crops shall be great and its winter will be severe. Princes shall be few, and those who govern silver and gold and all the things of this world shall be rare. The children of this world will retain their storerooms and barns and shall govern in the markets of buying and selling. Many shall be afflicted, and then they shall call upon their god that they might be delivered.[29] Happy they who are no longer alive at that time, as are they who are alive and endure. When all this comes about, then the one who is in labor shall soon give birth, since the time[30] is fulfilled."

9 "Then the son of perdition shall come, boasting and vaunting himself,[31] performing many signs and wonders[32] for the deception of the entire world. Happy are they who stay constant in those days, but woe to those who are led into deception."

[28]"Redeemed"; so the Cambridge-Paris fragment, supported by the Paris MS. Rahmani's text has "commanded."

[29]The Cambridge-Paris fragment has "my faithful ones shall be afflicted ... and shall call upon God." There is a translation error in this text in the course of the sentence.

[30]Or, following the Cambridge-Paris fragment and the Paris MS, "her time."

[31]2 Thess 2.4.

[32]2 Thess 2.9.

10 "Then Syria shall be a spoil of war and shall lament her children. Cilicia shall lift up her neck until the appearance of the one who shall judge her. For from her seat of glory there shall arise the daughter of Babylon to drink of the potion that has been mixed for her. Cappadocia, Lycia, Lycaonia shall bend their backs, as many multitudes shall be injured through their destructive wickedness. Then the camps of the barbarians shall lie open, as many chariots go forth to cover the earth. Through all of Armenia, Pontus, and Bithynia the young shall fall by the sword and their sons and daughters shall be led captive, whereas those of Lycaonia shall be mixed in blood. Pisidia, which was boastful and trusted in her riches, shall be razed to the ground. A sword shall pass through Phoenicia, for they are children of corruption. Judah shall clothe herself with lamentation, and shall prepare for the day of her destruction, on account of her impurity. Then shall she gather the abomination of desolation.[33] The east shall be opened up by him and the roads also shall be opened up by him. A sword and flame shall be in his hands, as he burns with anger and with the fire of his wrath. These are his weapons for the destruction of the children of earth, the elimination of the faithful and the way of bloodshed. For his way is error, his strength is blasphemy, his hand[34] is for deception, and his right hand is for disaster, and his left hand is for darkness."

11 "These are the signs which are his. His head is like a burning flame, his right eye is mixed with blood, his left is black and blue, as he has two pupils.[35] His eyebrows[36] are white, his lower lip is large

[33]Mt 24.15.

[34]The MSS all read singular, though given what follows a plural might make more sense.

[35]The Cambridge-Paris fragment and the Latin clarify that the left eye has two pupils. "He" may have referred to the eye, as *ophthalmos* (eye) is masculine in Greek.

[36]Eyebrows is taken from the Cambridge-Paris fragment and the Latin, as opposed to Rahmani's text, which reads "eyelashes." The reading seems likely since physiognomy, as practiced in the ancient world, would take eyebrows into account, but not, to my knowledge, lashes.

whilst his thigh is delicate and his feet are flat. His middle finger is bruised and flat. This is the sickle of desolation."[37]

12 "For this reason, children of light, it is I who say to you: the time is near and the harvest that is to be harvested with judgment is ripe. The judge shall arise to many as one who is kind, who will take account of what they have done. But when his coming is close at hand a sign shall be given to those elect who have kept my Father's law."

13 "Then those who fear my words and who perform them in truth with a faithful mind shall keep watch and pray without ceasing, reckoning it their duty to offer prayers at all times, not going astray in anything, nor wandering around this world, nor giving regard to anything, but with strong spirit and mind undoubting, bearing their cross daily, so that they may do the will of my Father in heaven with a humble heart. For the Lord is the one who has care and concern for those who put their trust in the truth, and he sends them whatever is fitting and right, those whom he knows and those he knows by his hands."

14 "I tell you these things so that, wherever you may go, you may test the souls in holiness and may speak to them of what is fitting and right and of what is to come, and whatever I commanded you before I was glorified, so that they may truly live whilst they remain faithful. For at this point comes about the beginning of trials, and the mystery of destruction.[38] Turn yourselves then to the church, setting her right and ordering and commanding what is proper, doing all things with righteousness and holiness. Speak to everybody what is profitable to them so that your Father who is in heaven may be glorified.[39] Be wise so that you may persuade those who are captivated by

[37]I argue in my "The Apocalyptic Section of *Testamentum Domini*: An Attempt at Dating," *Journal of Theological Studies* (ns) 62 (2011): 136–143, that this is a reference to the shape of the finger. "This" cannot refer to the finger in Syriac, but might in Greek.

[38]The Cambridge-Paris fragment concludes here.

[39]Mt 5.16.

error and those who are going around in ignorance, so that they may come to know God and, living in piety and purity, may give praise to my Father and your God."

15 After Jesus had spoken these words, Peter and John and Thomas and Matthias and Andrew and Matthew and the others said: "Lord, truly you have now spoken words of warning and of truth to us, and although we are unworthy you have granted us much and also given the grace to generations to come, who are worthy, that they may know your words and escape the snares of the evil one. But, Lord, we ask that your light should shine perfectly upon us and upon those who are foreordained and set apart as your own. Because we have asked so often, we beg you to teach us the proper nature of him who should stand at the head of the church, and with what rule[40] he should establish and order the church. For it is pressing that when we are sent to the gentiles to announce your salvation we should not be mistaken in the manner in which it is proper to manage the mysteries of the Church. Therefore, from your own voice, savior and perfecter, we desire to learn without omission how the leader in what is holy, and all those who minister within your church, should be pleasing towards you."

16 Then Martha, Mary, and Salome, who were with us, replied saying: "Lord, teach us indeed, so that we may know what is right for us to do so that our souls may live for you." Jesus answered them and said to them: "I desire that you should continue in intercession, that you should serve my gospel at all times, that you should show forth in yourselves a type of holiness for the salvation of those who patiently trust in me and that that in all things you should be likenesses of the kingdom of the heavens."

17 Yet Jesus also said to us: "Since you have also inquired concerning the ecclesiastical rule[41] I shall deliver it and make it known to

[40] *Kanōn* transliterated.
[41] *Kanōn* transliterated.

you in what manner it is right for you to order[42] and command him who stands at the head of the church and to keep the perfect and just and most excellent rule in which the Father who sent me is pleased. Truly I say to you, whoever knows the force of this commandment and of this testament and performs those things that are written therein shall be like to the angels who praise my Father and shall be sanctified to God.

My Father is a mediator and all of his host. So that should anyone whose sins are like the sand of the sea and cannot be numbered understand these words and perform them, his sins will be remitted and he will live in me and be glorified.[43]

18 Since there are increasingly many carnal desires in the midst of the assembly of the people, and the laborers are slight and few, the perfect labourers alone shall know the greater part of my words, all those that I spoke frequently to you in secret before I suffered, which you know. You both possess them and understand them, for my mysteries are given to those who are mine, together with whom I shall rejoice and be glad with my Father, who, after they are set free from life, shall come to me.

But these words that remain you should speak within the churches[44] when you have made them certain and established them.

From the day onward in which those who believe in me have the desire to know what is in this Testament, so that they may do what is of my Father, I shall be with them and will be glorified among them, and will have a habitation among them, making them recognize the will of my Father through my might.

As I have frequently commanded you, beware lest you give what is holy to the dogs, or lest you throw pearls before pigs.[45] Never give

[42] *Taxis* transliterated.

[43] "And be glorified" is supplied from the Synodicon text.

[44] The Synodicon text has a singular here.

[45] Mt 7.6. The text is similarly employed in Ps.-Athanasius, *On Virginity* 9 to refer to the virgins' secret practice of *askēsis*.

my holy things to those who are defiled and wicked and do not bear my cross, and who do not subject themselves. And my commandments shall be among them as a laughingstock. And for anyone who is embittered, and does not do them, and gives my words without gain, it shall be the destruction of their lives.

It is to be spoken and given over to those who are firm, fixed, and immovable, those who perform my commandments and this tradition, so that keeping them they may remain in me, sanctified, upright and strong, escaping any fall into evil and the death of sin as the Holy Spirit grants them grace to believe in the right way and spiritually to know what is of the Spirit by the Spirit, and to endure toil in hope, and to serve my gospel in joy, and to bear the mockery of my cross without doubt and with exultation. Since truly I say to you that those men who are so, and those women who are so, shall dwell, after the rest, in the third order[46] of my Father who sent me.[47]

19 I speak to you of how the sacred house should be, and then make known the holy rule[48] of the priests of the church.

A church should be thus: it should have three entrances as a representation of the Trinity.[49]

The deacons' house should be on the right of the entrance on the right so that they may observe the Eucharists, and the offerings that are offered. There should be a forecourt and a covered porch[50] going round to the deacons' house.

[46] *Taxis* transliterated.

[47] Cooper and Maclean suggest, the third heaven of 1 Cor 12.2. Cooper and Maclean, *Testament*, 148. The statement, however, seems to be clarified through the parallel in Ps.-Athanasius, *On Virginity* 10, in which it is said that those who read the treatise, and do what it teaches, will have their names written in the book of life and dwell in the third order (*tagma*) of the angels.

[48] *Kanōn* transliterated.

[49] Cf. the three gates to the east of Constantine's church of the Holy Sepulchre, described by Eusebius in *Life of Constantine* 3.37 and the triple entrance to the basilica at Tyre, described in the context of a speech of praise in *Church History* 10.4.41.

[50] *Stoa* transliterated.

Within the forecourt there should be a building as a building for baptism. Its length should be twenty-one cubits as a representation of the completion of the prophets, its width twelve cubits as a representation of those who are set down to proclaim the Gospel. It should have one entrance and three exits.

The church should have a house of catechumens, which is also a house of those who exorcize. This should not be separated from the church but should be such that those who enter may hear the readings and the spiritual songs and the psalms.

Then the throne should be set towards the east.[51] On the right and on the left should be the seats of the presbyters, so that those who are on the right are for those who are the more elevated and the more honored,[52] and those who labor in the word.[53] The left side is for those of middle age.

The setting of the throne should be lifted up three steps for it is proper that the altar should be so.

That house should have two covered porches, on the right and on the left, for the men and for the women.[54]

All the places should be illuminated, on account of a representation and on account of the reading.[55]

The altar should have a veil of pure linen, for it is without stain.[56] The house of baptism should likewise be under a veil.

[51]Reading, with Rahmani, and Ethiopic, *mdnha*, rather than the *mdbha* of the MSS, which would mean "the throne should be set beside the altar." See also 1.41 below.

[52]Thus observe that at Eusebius, *Church History* 10.4.44, the thrones of the basilica at Tyre are "higher up" and the seating is "in proper arrangement," for the honor of those who preside.

[53]Cf. 1 Tim 5.17.

[54]Cf., again, the double portico of Constantine's Holy Sepulchre, at *Life of Constantine* 3.37.

[55]Note, in the list of donations made by Constantine and his family to the Roman churches, preserved in the *Book of Pontiffs* (*Liber pontificalis*) 34.9–33, the regular occurrence of items such as candelabra, chandeliers, and candlesticks.

[56]It is worth observing that veils, as well as a throne and an altar, are listed among the furnishings of the church at Alexandria, destroyed in violence, mentioned by Athanasius, *History of the Arians* 56.

A building should be constructed as a place for commemoration. There the priest should be seated and the chief of the deacons, together with the readers, so that the names of those who offer offerings, or those on whose account they are offering, may be written down, so that when the holy gifts are being offered the reader or the chief of the deacons may name in commemoration those on whose account the priests and the people are making offering with supplication. For there is also such a representation in heaven.

The place of the presbyters should be within the veil, towards the place of commemoration.

The place for offerings and the treasury should be close to the house of the deacons.

However, the place for readings should be a little removed from the altar.

The house of the bishop should be close to that place that is called the forecourt. Likewise, also, that of the widows who are called preeminent. Likewise also that of the presbyters and deacons should be beyond the house of baptism. The deaconesses, however, should remain near the gate of the Lord's house.

A house of hospitality, in which the chief of the deacons may receive strangers, should be close to the church.

20 After the house is as is becoming and right a bishop should be appointed. He should be chosen by all the people in accordance with the will of the Holy Spirit. He should be faultless, chaste, gentle, humble, free of anxiety, watchful, not a lover of money, blameless, not contentious, merciful, learned, not talkative, a lover of what is good, a lover of labor, a lover of the widows, a lover of the orphans, a lover of the poor, who is familiar with the mysteries, not lax or fond of this world's company, who is peaceable, perfect in all that is good, as one to whom the position and the place of God is entrusted. It is good if he is without wife, but should at least be the husband of one wife so that he may sympathize with the weakness of the widows. When he is appointed he should be of middle age, not a youth.[57]

21 When there is somebody like this he shall receive the imposition of a hand on the first day of the week, with all agreeing to his appointment and bearing witness to him, together with all the presbyters and the bishops who are in attendance.[58]

These bishops should lay hands upon him, washing their hands beforehand. The presbyters should stand by them in silence, in fear, while lifting up their hearts in quietness.

After that the bishops should lay hands upon him while they say: "We lay hands upon a servant of God who has been elected in the Spirit for the firm and devoted[59] ordering[60] of the Church, whose headship is united and indissoluble, the invisible living God, for the delivery of true judgment and of divine and sacred revelations, and of divine gifts and of faithful teaching of the Trinity, by means of the cross, by means of the resurrection, by means of the incorruption, in the sacred Church of God."

After this, one of the of the bishops, commanded by the other bishops, should lay hands upon him, while he says the following statement of appointment:

The Prayer for the Ordination[61] of a Bishop

God who do all things in strength, who establish them,
who have founded the inhabited world with reason,
who have decorated the crown of all the things that you made,
who gave us your commandments so that we might serve you
in fear,

[57] To this list of qualifications cf. those of the Pastoral Epistles (1 Tim 3.2–7 and Tit 1.6–9). They are taken up elsewhere in the church order literature, notably in the *Didascalia of the Apostles* and the *Apostolic Church Order*. See, moreover, discussion of this point in the introduction.

[58] Or "neighboring bishops."

[59] *Eusebēs* transliterated.

[60] *Katastasis* transliterated.

[61] Cheirotonia transliterated.

who have bequeathed to us the understanding of the truth,
who made known to us the goodness of your Spirit,
and who sent your beloved Son as our sole savior, spotless for our redemption,
God and Father of our Lord Jesus Christ,
Father of compassion and God of all consolation,
who dwell eternally on high in purity,
you who are the most high, praiseworthy, fearful, great, all-seeing,
who know everything before it comes about,
with whom were all things before they existed,
who have given illumination to the church[62] by means of the goodness of your only begotten Son,
who determined beforehand, from the beginning, those who would delight in the just and act in holiness, and so dwell in your habitations,
who chose Abraham who pleased you in faith,
who translated the sainted Enoch to the treasure-house of life,
who ordain princes and priests for your holy house on high, Lord,
who call them to praise and glorify your holy name and your only begotten in the place of your glory:
Lord God, you have not left your exalted sanctuary without ministry since before the foundation of the world and have, since the foundation of the world, adorned and glorified your sanctuary with faithful princes and priests after the likeness of your own heavens.
You, Lord, are pleased to be praised even now, and have granted that there should be princes for your people.
Give illumination, pour forth understanding and the grace of your governing Spirit that you passed on to your beloved Son Jesus Christ.

[62]"To the church" is omitted in the Synodicon text.

Give wisdom, O God, give reason, fortitude, strength, unity in the Spirit in doing all things working with you.
Grant your Spirit, holy God, which was given to your holy one, sending it on your holy and pure Church and on every place that sings of your holiness.
And grant, Lord, that this your servant should please you in telling of your glory,
in unceasing praise, O God,
in fitting hymns of glorification and in suitable occasions,[63]
in acceptable prayers,
in faithful supplication,
in right thinking,
in a humble heart,
in life's activity,
in humility and in truth,
in knowledge of what is right.
Father, you know the heart:
may this, your servant, chosen for the episcopate, feed your holy flock and stand without fault at the head of the priesthood,
ministering day and night.
Grant that he may see your face,[64] and that he may offer to you the offerings of your holy Church with care and all fearfulness.
Confer on him the empowering spirit that is yours, as you conferred it on your apostles, that he may loosen every bond.
So that he may please you in all humility, fill him with love, knowledge, understanding, discipline, completion of growth, fortitude, and purity of heart
when he prays for the people

[63]Cooper and Maclean, *Testament*, 67n4, suggest that "fitting and opportune hymns" might have been the underlying Greek.
[64]*Prosōpon* transliterated.

and when he grieves with those who have gone astray[65] and
brings to them assistance,
when he offers you praises and thanksgivings and prayers as a
sweet-smelling savor[66]
through your beloved Son, our Lord Jesus Christ,
through whom to you be praise and honor and might together
with the Holy Spirit
before the worlds, and now, and for all time and to the ages of
the endless ages. Amen.

And the people should say "Amen." And then cry out: "He is worthy, he is worthy, he is worthy."

Afterwards the people should keep the feast for three days in accordance with the mystery of him who after three days arose from the house of the dead.

Everyone then should give him the peace.

22 He should be constant at the altar. He should persist in prayer, day and night, especially at the required times in the night, at the first hour, in the middle of the night, and at earliest dawning when the day star appears, and again in the morning at the third hour, the sixth, the ninth, and the twelfth hour of the lamp.[67] He does well if he offers prayer without ceasing at every hour on behalf of the people and on behalf of himself. He should exclusively be in the house of the church. If, however, there be one or two of like spirit with him it is right that he should be with them for supplication with a single voice. For when two or three are gathered in my name you know that I have said to you that I will be among them.[68] If, however, he is unable to

[65]For "those who have gone astray" the Synodicon text reads "those who suffer."

[66]Eph 5.8.

[67]Cf. to this provision those of the *Longer Rule* of Basil 37.2–5, noted by Grant White, *Daily Prayer and its Ascetic Context in the Syriac and Ethiopic* Testamentum Domini (Joensuu: University of Joensuu, 2002), 127. Note also the *horarium* at 2.24 below.

[68]Beyond the reference to Mt 18.20, note the similar provision for widows at 1.40 below and the note ad loc.

remain for the whole night in its entirety he should remain for those hours of which I have spoken. For then the angels visit the church.

He should fast for three days throughout the year.[69] For three weeks after his appointment he should observe the fast according to the number of the eighteen exalted entrances through which the only begotten passed when he came to the passion.[70] On the first [day] of the week only, however, he should feed on bread with oil and honey and salt and all fruits of the trees. But he should not taste wine at all, apart from the cup of the offering alone. This he should use whether well or ill, for it is right that this should be exclusively for the priests. And so, after this, he should fast for three days throughout the year. For the rest of the time he should fast according to his ability. But he should not eat meat at all. Not because he is blameworthy if he tastes or eats it but because such strong meats are unfitting to one who loves weakness, and in order that he might keep vigil.[71]

There should be an offering on every Sabbath and[72] every Sunday and on the day of fasting. In the evening,[73] he should instruct and teach the mysteries to those who have been tested as having ears to hear.

[69]That is to say, he is to fast for three days weekly, the same provision being made for the presbyter at 1.31 below.

[70]This expression is obscure. However, Cooper and Maclean, *Testament*, 162, observe 18 entrances made by Jesus in Luke.

[71]This qualification of episcopal vegetarianism may be read in the light of the second canon of Gangra, which states that somebody who eats meat is not to be condemned on that basis.

[72]The text has "or." I have emended ʾ*w* (or) to *w* (and), on the basis of logic and on the basis of the statements at 1.23. The Ethiopic also reads "or," but the words are the same as Syriac, and so the same error might easily occur. Canon 49 of the Council of Laodicea restricts eucharistic celebrations in Lent to the Sabbath and Sunday.

[73]Or "There should be an offering on every Sabbath and every Sunday. And on the day of fasting, in the evening, he should instruct." I have translated above (with Rahmani, and in opposition to Nau) because this is the understanding of the Borgian Arabic (which has "on each feast day occurring during the week"), and, fundamentally, because, on the assumption that the fast days are Wednesday and Friday, we may observe that these are the days on which Basil communicated (that is to say, Sunday, Wednesday, Friday, and the Sabbath) (Basil, *Letter* 93, to Caesaria.) Ethiopic may hold the clue, rendering: "There should be an offering on every Sabbath and every Sunday, and on the day of fasting when, in the evening, he should instruct."

Should he have some bodily infirmity he should be concerned to heal himself speedily, feeding on fish and constantly taking a little of the wine of the offering so that the church does not cease to function on account of his lying sick and so that those who learn the word may delight.

When he is teaching in the church he should speak carefully, as a man who recognizes that he is speaking in witness to the teaching of the whole ministry of the Father of all, which is accurately written. He should speak all this, all that he knows and all that he recalls from beforehand. If he speaks of what he knows he may be hopeful that his hearers likewise will come to understanding. He should beseech the Lord in all his labor that the fruit of the Holy Spirit may come about in all his hearers.

Let everything be done in good order and with knowledge.

He should dismiss the catechumens after admonishing them with directions and exhortations with prophetic and apostolic teaching, so that they should know the Lord whom they have confessed. To the faithful, however, he should teach the mysteries, previously having dismissed the catechumens, and then should offer the mystery after instruction, so that they may approach in fear and be aware of the mystery in which they are participating.

23 On the Sabbath day three loaves are offered as a sign of the Trinity; on the Sunday, however, as a sign of the Gospels, four loaves are offered. Because the former people erred, the curtain of the entrance should be closed while he makes the offering. Within the veil he should be offering with the presbyters and the deacons and the canonical widows and the subdeacons and the women deacons and the readers (and) those who have charisms.[74] The bishop should be standing foremost in the center, and the presbyters immediately behind him on either side. The widows should be immediately behind the presbyters on the left-hand side and the deacons likewise

[74]The presence of women behind the veil is noteworthy, as the canons of Laodicea expressly forbid the presence of women close to the altar (Canon 44). In the introduction, we noted that the *Testament* stands in tension to these canons (see p. 57).

behind the presbyters on the right-hand side. The readers should be behind them and the subdeacons behind the readers and the deaconesses behind the subdeacons. The bishop should lay his hand on the loaves that have been set on the altar and the presbyters lay their hands together with him, and the rest simply stand there.

The loaf of a catechumen shall not be accepted, even should he have a son or a wife who is a believer and wishes it to be offered on their behalf. The offering is not made unless he is baptized. Before the bishop or the presbyter makes the offering the people should give the peace to each other.

Afterwards, when there is a great silence, the deacon should say:

The Proclamation of the Deacon upon the Eucharist[75]

Your hearts in heaven!
If anyone is in anger with his neighbor he should be reconciled.
If anyone has conscience of lack of faith he should confess it.
If anyone has a thought contrary to the commandments he should depart.
If anyone has fallen into sin he should not hide. For it is not possible to conceal himself.[76]
If anyone has a disordered reason he should not approach.
If anyone is impure, if anyone is not steadfast, he should give up his place.
If anyone is a stranger to the commandments of Jesus he should depart.
If anyone despises the prophets he should separate himself. He should deliver himself from the wrath of the only begotten.
Let us not despise the cross.
Let us flee the threat.
We have the Lord looking on, the Father of lights with the Son, the angels visiting.

[75]*Eucharistia* transliterated.
[76]Or, less probably, "it is not possible to conceal it," though note Psalm 69.5.

Examine yourselves lest you be in dispute with your neighbor.
Look, lest anyone should be in a state of anger, as God will see it.
Lift up your hearts for the offering for the salvation of life and of holiness.
In the wisdom of God let us accept the grace which has been given us.

After this, the bishop should speak, giving and rendering thanks with an awed voice:

"Our Lord be with you."
The people should say: "And also with your spirit."
The bishop should say: "Lift up your hearts."
The people should say: "We have them to the Lord."
The bishop should say: "Let us give thanks to the Lord."
The people should say: "It is right and just."
The bishop should say: "Holy things for holy people."[77]
The people should say: "In heaven and on earth without ceasing."

[77]On the basis of a version of the anaphora of the *Testamentum* preserved in Arabic in the *Nomocanon* of Macarius, Anton Baumstark, "Die arabischen Texte der *Diathēkē tou Kuriou*," *Römische Quartalschrift* 14 (1900): 291–300, at 298, suggested that the original here read "Holy, Holy, Holy is the Lord of hosts, in heaven and on earth, for ever and ever." This is plausible, and fits better with the people's response than the present text. The reading is, moreover, supported by the Arabic edited by Gérard Troupeau, "Une version arabe de l'anaphore du *Testamentum Domini*," in *Christianisme Oriental: Kérygme et Histoire; Mélanges Offerts au Père Michel Hayek*, ed. Charles Chartouni (Paris: Librairie orientaliste Paul Geuthner, 2007), 247–256. However, Troupeau suggests (at "Version Arabe," 255) that the insertion of the *Sanctus* here is the action of the scribe, unfamiliar with the *Sancta sanctis* in this position. As in the words over the cup below, where I have preferred the Arabic reading, we cannot have certainty either way. In both instances the Ethiopic is in agreement with the Syriac.

The Eucharist,[78] *or Thanksgiving over the Offerings*[79]

And straightaway the bishop should say:

"We render thanks to you, O God, who are holy,
the strengthener of our souls, and giver of grace,
treasury of incorruption and Father of your only begotten our savior,
whom in these recent times you have sent to us as savior and proclaimer of your purpose.
For it is your purpose that we should be saved in you.
Our heart gives thanks to you, Lord, our mind, our soul with all its understanding,
so that your grace may come upon us, Lord,
so that we may praise you ceaselessly,
and your only begotten Son and the Holy Spirit, now and forever and to the age of the ages. Amen.

You are the strength of the Father,
the grace of the nations,
knowledge, true wisdom,
the lifting-up of the lowly, the healing of the soul,[80] the confidence of us who are faithful,
for you are the strength of the righteous,
the hope of those who are persecuted,
the haven of those who are afflicted,
the enlightener of the perfect,
the Son of the living God.

[78] *Eucharistia* transliterated.

[79] Reading a plural with the Mosul MS. Other MSS read a singular, and Rahmani makes the correction. However, the provisions for receiving offerings in the place of commemoration, the reference to plural offerings in the deacons' house (both at 1.19 above) and the provisions concerning the receipt of offerings from catechumens all indicate that a plural is possible. The title is not found in the Ethiopic.

[80] Here accepting Rahmani's correction, now supported by the Ethiopic. The Syriac MSS read: "the healing of the humble, the lifting up of souls."

From your gifts of immeasurable greatness cause courage, fortitude, confidence, wisdom, constancy, unswerving faith, unfailing hope, knowledge of your spirit, lowliness, uprightness, to shine forth upon us,
so that we your servants and all your people may always glorify you in purity, may bless you, may give thanks to you, Lord, at all times, and entreat you."

Again the bishop should say:

"You, Lord, are the founder of the heights,
the king of the treasury of lights,
the overseer of the heavenly Sion,
the king of the ranks of archangels, of dominions, of praises, of thrones, of clothing, of lights, of rejoicings, of delights,
you hold all things in your hand,
you sustain all things in your reason,
through your only begotten Son who was crucified for our sins.
You, Lord, sent your Word,
Son of your mind and Son of your statute,
by whom you made all that is,
with whom you were well pleased,
into a virgin womb.
He was seen as your Son, conceived and enfleshed,
when he was born of the Holy Spirit and the virgin.
Fulfilling your will and preparing a holy people he opened his hands for suffering so that he might set free from suffering and from corruption and death those who put their hope in you.
When he was handed over to voluntary suffering
so that he might set upright those who had slipped,
and find those who were lost,
and give life to the dead,
and dissolve death,
and unbind the chains of the devil,

and complete the Father's will,
and tread down Sheol,
and open the way of life,
and guide the righteous to light,
and to fix a boundary,
and illuminate the darkness,
and increase the children,
and show forth the resurrection,
then he took bread.
He gave it to his disciples and said: 'Take, eat. This is my body, which is broken for you for the forgiveness of sins. Whenever you do this you make my memorial.'[81]
And he mixed the cup of wine, blessed it, and gave it to them saying: 'Take, drink from this, all of you. This is my blood which is poured out for you.' "[82]

And again he should say:

"Thus remembering your death and resurrection we offer to you bread and cup as we give thanks to you.

[81]Syr. *qymtʾ* is translated previously as "resurrection." However, with different pointing the same word means an obelisk or memorial stone. I therefore suggest that the translator has employed the term to render "commemoration," an unusual usage that has misled modern translators. Arabic texts available, and Ethiopic, also have "commemoration." W. E. Pitt, "Anamnesis and Institution Narrative in the Liturgy of *Apostolic Constitutions* 8," *JEH* 9 (1958): 1–7, at 5, suggests that this came about through a misreading of *anamnēsis* (memorial) as *anastasis* (resurrection), a suggestion I accepted earlier.

[82]After consideration I give the text here after the Arabic edited by Troupeau. Cf. Syriac: "Likewise the cup of wine, which he mixed, he gave as a type of the blood which was shed for us." Ligier, "Anaphore," 99, with reference to anaphoras studied by A. Raes, "Les Paroles de la Consécration dans les Anaphoras Syriennes," *OCP* 3 (1937): 484–504, suggests that the abbreviated version of the words over the cup found in the Syriac text of this anaphora has a similarity to certain medieval Syrian anaphoras that also abbreviate the words of Jesus at the last supper. This is not entirely accurate, as these later anaphoras do not abbreviate in the same way, and are similarly free with the words over the bread. Rahmani, *Testamentum*, 43, by contrast, considers this a manifest error. It is possible that it is deliberate scribal alteration, though we cannot have complete assurance on the point. The Ethiopic supports the Syriac.

You alone are God forever, and savior to us, because you have made us worthy[83] to stand before you and to minister to you as a priest.
On this account we your servants give thanks to you, Lord."

And the people should speak in a similar fashion.

Again he should say:

"To you do we offer this thanksgiving, eternal Trinity,
O Lord Jesus Christ,
O Lord the Father, from whom every creature and every nature escapes into itself in trembling.
O Lord the Holy Spirit, send some of your holiness onto this drink and this food,[84]
cause that it should not be for our condemnation,
nor for our reproach,
nor for our destruction,
but for the healing and strengthening of our spirit.
Grant, Lord, through your name, that every thought should flee that is not pleasing to you.
Grant, Lord, that every thought of pride should be driven from us by means of your name,
which is written within the faces of the gate of your holy heights,
which causes Sheol to be stunned when it hears it,
the depth is rent,
spirits are driven away,
the serpent is crushed,
unbelief is banished,

[83]Syr. reads *ʾstwdyt* (promised). *ʾswyt* (counted worthy), a reading borne out by subsequently discovered versions of *Apostolic Tradition*, was suggested by Rahmani, *Testamentum*, 42, though Cooper and Maclean, *Testament*, 73, continue to maintain "promise," translating "Thou hast promised to us to stand before Thee." The Ethiopic reads "commanded."

[84]For a justification of the translation offered here, see the appendix to the introduction.

disobedience is subdued,
anger is quieted,
envy is rendered ineffective,
arrogance is reproved,
love of money is rooted out,
vainglory is removed,
pride is humbled,
all cause of bitterness[85] is driven away.
So grant, Lord, that our inward eyes may perceive you,
praise you, glorify you, recall you, serve you, have part with you alone, Son and Word of God,
to whom all things are subject.
Sustain to the end those with the grace of revelation.
Confirm those with the grace of healing.
Give courage to those with the power of tongues.
Keep upright those with a word of instruction.
Take care of those who do your will at all times, visit the widows, assist the orphans.
Remember those who have gone to rest in the faith.
Grant us an inheritance with your saints,
and grant us the grace of pleasing you just as they were pleasing to you.
Shepherd the people in uprightness, and sanctify us all, O God.
But grant that all of those who participate and receive of your holy things may be united with you, so being filled with your Holy Spirit for the confirmation of the faith in truth
that they may speak your praise forever,
and to your beloved Son Jesus Christ
as through him to you is praise and might, together with the Holy Spirit, forever and ever."

The people should say: "Amen."

[85]Here reading *mrr*ʾ (bitterness), rather than the *mr*ʾ (master) of the MSS. The Ethiopic reads "bitterness."

The deacon: Let us earnestly entreat our Lord and God that he might bestow on us a spirit of harmonious concord.
The bishop: Grant harmonious concord by the Holy Spirit, and save our souls by means of this offering, so that we may live with you for all the ages of the ages.
The people: Amen.

The people also repeat as they pray.

And when all this is done the seal of the thanksgiving thus: "Blessed be the name of the Lord forever."

The people: Amen.
The priest: "Blessed is the one who has come in the name of the Lord. Blessed the name of his glory." And let all the people say: "So be it. So be it."
The bishop should say: "Send the grace of the spirit upon us."

The bishop should not offer if he has ejaculated in a dream,[86] but a presbyter should offer. Likewise he should not partake of the mysteries, not as though he were polluted but out of respect for the altar.[87] When he has fasted and bathed in pure water he may draw near and minister. In the same manner for a presbyter. Moreover if a widow is menstruating she should not draw near. In the same way any other woman, or a layman, or anyone else of the orders, should not approach out of respect except after fasting and bathing.

The priests should receive first,[88] thus: The bishop, the presbyters, the deacons, the widows, the readers, the subdeacons. Afterwards those who have spiritual gifts, the newly baptized, infants. The people thus: the elderly, celibates, and then the rest. The women so: the deaconesses first and then the others.

[86]Literally, "has been in a dream of coition."

[87]This qualification may be made in view of the hyper-asceticism that the Synod of Gangra sought to control, or may be made in the light of the insistence on ritual cleansing on the basis of discerning pollution made by some Christians of Jewish practice, who are opposed rigorously in the *Didascalia of the Apostles.*

[88]The Synodicon text omits the reference to priests.

Everyone who receives the thanksgiving should say "Amen" before partaking. Afterwards he should pray thus. After he receives of the Eucharist he should say:

"Holy, Holy, Holy, Ineffable Trinity,
grant to me that I should receive this body for life, and not for condemnation.
And grant to me that I should bear fruit that pleases you
so that, when I am seen to be pleasing to you I may live in you, performing your commandments,
and call you 'Father' with boldness when I call upon your kingdom and your will.
May your name be sanctified in me, Lord, since you are powerful and glorious, and yours is the glory unto the ages. Amen."

And he should take when he has prayed.

When he partakes from the chalice he should say "Amen" a second time[89] for the completion of the body and the blood.

When everybody has received they should pray, rendering and giving thanks for having received, as the deacon calls out: "Let us render thanks to the Lord that we have received these holy things so that this reception should be for the life and salvation of our souls. Let us beg and beseech, raising a word of glorification to the Lord God."

And afterwards the bishop:

"O Lord, giver of eternal light,
pilot of souls, guide of saints,
give us eyes of understanding that look upon you at all times and ears that hear only you,
that our soul may be filled with your grace.
Set a pure heart within us, O God,[90] that at all times we may understand your greatness.

[89]Or "say 'amen' twice."
[90]Ps 51.10.

O wonderful God, loving towards people,
improve our souls and form our thoughts that they may be undeviating,
by means of this Eucharist[91] in which we, your inadequate servants, have partaken.
For blessed is your kingdom, Lord God, glorious and uplifted, in the Father and in the Son and in the Holy Spirit from before time and now and for all times and for the ages, and for the unending ages."

The people: Amen.

24 If the priest consecrates oil for the healing of those who suffer, he should say quietly, as he places that vessel on the altar:

"Lord God, you have bestowed on us the Spirit, the Paraclete, the Lord, the saving and steadfast name, which is hidden from the foolish but revealed to the wise, Christ who sanctifies us,
and through your kindness to us you make us, your servants whom you have chosen, wise with the wisdom that is yours,
you have sent the knowledge of your Spirit to us sinners through the holiness that is yours, as you grant us the grace of your Spirit;
you are the healer of all sickness and all suffering,
you gave the gift of healing to those counted worthy by you:
send out upon this oil, which is the representation of your fatness, the deliverance of your good compassion,
that it may deliver those who labor,
heal those who are sick,
and sanctify those who return when they approach your faith.
Since the power is yours and the glory forever."

The people: Amen.

[91] *Eucharistia* transliterated.

25 In the same manner, likewise, also over water.

26 At the earliest dawning the bishop should gather the people so that the service might be completed at the rising of the sun. When he says the first hymn of praise for the dawn, as the presbyters approach, and the deacons, and the rest of the faithful, he should say thus:

"Glory to the Lord."
And the people should say: "It is right and just."

Hymn of Praise for the Dawn

The bishop: "It is right and just that we should glorify and praise and thank you, ineffable God, who made all things.
As we stretch our souls upward we lift a morning hymn of praise to you, Lord, to you who are all-wise, mighty and most merciful God, the strength and protector of our souls.
We praise you, O Word which was before the ages, begotten of the Father,
who rejoice solely in your saints,
who are glorified in the hymns of the archangels
to you, the maker not made by hands, and declarer of holy things invisible, pure and without spot,
to you who make known to us hidden mysteries of wisdom and promise us the light of immortality,
to you, Lord, we your servants lift up a pure and holy hymn of glory."

The people should say:

"We glorify you, we bless you, we give thanks to you, O Lord, and entreat you, our God."

Once again, the bishop:

"God, the begetter of light,
the source of life,

the giver of knowledge,
the gift of grace,
the maker of souls making whatever is beautiful,
giver of the Holy Spirit,
treasury of wisdom,
maker of whatever is good,
Lord, teacher of holiness,
holding the worlds by your will,
receiving prayers that are pure,
to you we give glory.
Only begotten Son,
firstborn and Word of the Father,
who bestow all graces upon us who call upon you for help, and
  to the Father who begot you.
You, whose essence is imperishable, which neither moth nor
  worm may corrupt,
you who give to those who trust in you with all their heart those
  things which angels long to look upon,
who are the guardian of everlasting light, the incorruptible
  treasury,
who enlightened the darkness within us by the will of your
  Father,
who have borne us from the depth into the light,
who have given us life instead of death,
who have bestowed upon us freedom instead of slavery,
who by your cross have brought us home to your Father,
who by your gospel have led us to the heights of the heavens,
who by means of your prophets have comforted us,[92]
who by means of your own self have brought us home to the
  Father of lights,

[92]So Rahmami's Syriac. However, this is surely a translation of *parakaleō*, which would be better translated "exhort."

grant, Lord, that we may glorify you, our God, forever, so that we, your servants, with unceasing thanksgiving, may tell out your glory."

The people: "We glorify you, we bless you, we give thanks to you, we entreat you, our God."

Again the bishop should say:

"This threefold hymn of praise we make to you with our mouths, in the likeness of your kingdom,
Son of God,
who are of eternity,
who are above all with the Father,
whom all creation glorifies, trembling with fear of your Spirit,
before whom every nature trembles,
and whom every soul of the righteous ones blesses.
To you do we all flee for succour,
you assuage all disturbance, tempests, and winds for us,
you are a haven of rest for us and a place of refuge from corruption,
upon whom is our hope for eternal salvation,
who make fine weather for those who are battered on the seas and in the storms,
you are entreated in sickness and freely heal,
you are present with those imprisoned,
you have set us free from the bonds of death,
consoler of the poor and of those who grieve, and of those who have labored and exhausted themselves with the cross,
you avert from us every threat,
you have confounded Satan's tricks on our behalf, driving away every threat of his, and yourself granting courage to us,
you drive away every error from those who put their trust in you.
The prophets and apostles praised you secretly.

We praise you, Lord, we lift up our hymn of praise to you.
Since we have come to know you, through yourself, let us find rest in the dwellings of the living,
doing your will forever.
Grant, Lord, that we may walk in accordance with your commandments,
visit us with mercy,
the great and the insignificant alike,
the prince and his people,
the shepherd and his flock,
for you, Lord, are our God, and blessed and praised is your Kingdom,
of the Father and the Son and the Holy Spirit,
as it was before the ages, is now, and always, and to the generations and the unending ages."

The people: Amen.

They should sing psalms and four canticles, one that is by Moses, and of Solomon, and from the other prophets, thus: the boys who sing psalms, two virgins, three deacons, three presbyters. And likewise a hymn of praise should be said by the bishop, or by one of the presbyters in this way.

It should be said thus: "May the grace of the Lord be with you all."

And the people should say: "And with your spirit."
And the priest should say: "Again let us praise our Lord."
And the people should say: "It is right and just."
And the priest should say: "Let your hearts be fixed."
And the people should say: "We have them in the presence of the Lord."

Concluding Hymn of Praise[93]

Lord, Father,
giver of light,
origin of power and of all spirits,
seal of eternal light and guide of life,
maker of delight and immortality,
you made us so that we might pass through material darkness
and bestowed immaterial light upon us,
you release the chains of disobedience,
you crown the faith that is yours,
you do not distance yourself from your own servants, but are with them at all times,
you do not disregard those who entreat you with effort and reverence,
you know everything before it is considered,
you examine everything before it is thought,
you are gracious in giving before you are asked,
you are well pleased to hear those who worship you with an undivided mind,
king of the leading luminaries and hosts of heaven,
you hear the praises of the archangels and find rest in them:
hear us, Lord, who call upon you,
and grant that we may praise you without ceasing with all our hearts.
We exult you, we lift up a hymn of glory to you,
so that, we, your servants, may praise you without ceasing,
being guarded by you and guided by light.

[93]Or "hymn of praise for the seal." White, *Daily Prayer,* 140, believes that there was a liturgical act here demarcating the liturgical acts. His evidence lies in the Ethiopic, which states here: "The priest says this, after the sign of the cross." However, given that the majority of Ethiopic manuscripts do not have this title, it is possible that the translator had misunderstood the word *sphragis* (the Syriac is *hwtm*), and created this "signing" out of the title. The one Ethiopic MS with a title has "morning hymn," which may be an attempt to create a title given its absence.

The people: We glorify you, we bless you, we give thanks to you,
O Lord, we entreat you, our God.

The priest: Holy Lord Jesus, hear us.
You who are the voice of the mute and those without reason,
the support of the paralyzed,
the enlightener of the blind,
the guide of the weak,
the cleanser of the lepers,
the curer of the fluxes of nature,
the healer of the deaf, the reprover of death,
the torturer of darkness,
the dazzling of light and inextinguishable lamp,
the inextinguishable sun that rests not, but which shines forth
always through your saints,
you have brought all things into one to form beauty,
you are the rationale of good order,[94]
you have brightly shone on all,
you are the savior of humanity and the converter of souls,
you, as is right, are provider of all,
you are the maker of the angels and the mind of the Father,
you established the worlds with understanding and wisdom,
and made them firm in unity,
and were sent to us from your eternal Father,
you are the intellect of the incomprehensible and inexplicable
spirit,
you make known what is invisible,
you are glorious and your name is revered.
Therefore we too, your servants, praise you.

The people: We glorify you, we bless you, we give thanks to you,
O Lord, we entreat you, our God.

[94]Cooper and Maclean, *Testament*, 83, suggest that this renders *eukrasia*.

The priest: Holy Lord, this threefold hymn of praise we make to you,
who have given us an indissoluble faith in you, by means of which we might overcome the chains of death.
You created understanding minds for those who put their trust in you, so that they might become gods,
you promised that we might tread the power of the enemy underfoot through the power of the Spirit, so that he should not profane those things that are not to be profaned.
By means of your mediation you have brought about our friendship with your Father.
Answer us, your servants, Lord, who pray to you without ceasing.
You gave us power against the enemy at our request;
we beseech you at all times for the destruction of the evil one.
Hear us, eternal king:
comfort the widows,
assist the orphans,
have pity on those possessed by unclean spirits and purify them,
give wisdom to the foolish,
put right those who are wandering,
set free those in prison,
keep watch over us all,
for you, Lord, are our God, whose Kingdom is blessed and glorified.

The people: Amen.

27 After this the prayer should be completed. Then the reader should read the prophets, and the rest. The presbyter or the deacon should read the Gospel. Afterwards the bishop or the presbyter should teach whatever is suitable or beneficial. Next there should be a prayer, and the catechumens should receive a laying on of a hand.

28 After this the bishop instructs the people in the mysteries. If he is not present[95] the presbyter should speak so that the faithful may know the one whom they are approaching, and who is God and Father to them.

The instruction in the mysteries should be delivered in this way:

The Presentation of the Mysteries That Is to Be Addressed to the Faithful Prior to the Offering

He who was in the beginning, is now, and who is to come,
who suffered, was buried, who rose,
who is glorified by the Father,
who set free our cords from death,
who rose from the dead,
who is human and at the same time also is God,
who by means of the Holy Spirit restored the flesh of Adam, with his soul, to immortality,
since he conserved Adam in the spirit.[96]
He clothed himself in dead Adam and caused him to live.
He ascended into heaven,
and death fell beneath him, and was conquered, after the cross,
when the chains, by which the adversary had grown strong and from time to time prevailed against us, were loosened.
By his passion he (the devil) was shown to be powerless and weak,
when he cut his ropes and his power,
when his snares were snapped,
when he struck him on the face.[97]
He who was full of darkness was alarmed and fearful when he saw the only begotten Son descending into Sheol with the life of his divinity.

[95]Lit. "Nearby."
[96]Or "by the Spirit."
[97]*Prosōpon* transliterated.

He descended from the highest realms, beyond heaven,
he who is the indivisible thought of the Father, and is co-equal in will with him.
With his Father he formed the heavens,
he is the crown of the angels,
the strength of the archangels,
the clothing of the powers
and the spirit of the dominions.
He is ruler of the everlasting kingdom,
the head of the saints,
and the incomprehensible mind of the Father.
He is wisdom,
he is strength,
he is Lord,
he is understanding,
the intellect, the hand, the arm of the Father.
As we believe, so we confess,
he is our light, salvation, savior, protector, helper, teacher, deliverer, rewarder, assistance, strength, wall.
He is our shepherd, entrance, door, way, life, medicine, food, drink, judge.
We confess him passible and impassible,
uncreated Son,
dead (yet) living, Son of the Father,
incomprehensible and comprehensible.
He bore our sins, he who was without sin, when he came forth from the Father's heaven.
His body, broken, was our salvation
and his blood and Spirit life and sanctification,
the water our purification.
He enlightens[98] the hearts of those who fear him, being with them in all things.

[98]Reading, with Rahmani, *dmnhr* (who enlightens). The MSS have *dmnh*, which does not make much sense. Cooper and Maclean, *Testament*, 184, suggest, as an alter-

He has made us strangers to every way of the adversary.
He restores the souls of all of us who have put our trust in him.
He was God, and was from before the ages with the Father;
he saw the world perishing in the bonds of sin,
crushed by the power of a cunning wild beast,
subject to death through ignorance and error,
he determined to heal the human race,
he entered the womb of a virgin,
hidden from all the heavenly dwellings
and casting all the opposing powers into ignorance.
However, when he, who was incorruptible,
clothed himself in corruptible flesh,
he made flesh that was under death to be incorruptible,
he showed, in the flesh of the dead Adam, in which he clothed himself,
a type of incorruptibility, and so, in a type, put to an end whatever is corruptible.
He delivered cleansing commandments by means of the gospel,
which is the prior proclamation of his kingdom,
and through the gospel we have learnt to live as a sign of the kingdom,
and through this same gospel the chains of the adversary are sundered,
so that we may attain immortality instead of death,
and obtain watchfulness instead of ignorance.
Thus the one who became human is the Son of the Lord God,
who took the mortal race[99] of Adam in its forms[100] through self-emptying.
He who was eternal came to birth,

native, *dmnyh* (who take delight in), a reading from a version of the *Testament* called the Arabic *Didascalia*. Both are possible, as "enlighten" is the reading of the Borgian Arabic, whereas "take delight" is read by the Bohairic. Nonetheless the Ethiopic supports Rahmani's emendation.

[99] *Genos* transliterated.

[100] *Eidos* transliterated.

the one who was God was human.
He was made known by the prophets in advance,
he was proclaimed by the apostles,
he was extolled by the angels,
and glorified by the Father of all.[101]
He was crucified on our account;
his cross is life for us,
strength and salvation for us,
it is the hidden mystery,
the ineffable joy,
and through it the whole human nature is made inseparable from God, through bearing it at all times.
It is the merciful grace, inseparable from God, of which these lips cannot worthily speak.
It was hidden from the beginning, but now the mystery is revealed,
and so it is present to the faithful, not in appearance but in reality.
This is the cross, in which we glory so that we may be glorified.
We, the faithful who bear it, are perfected by it,
separating our selves from all that is perceptible,
all that is visible,
from all that is not true.
You who think yourselves mighty, make your visible ears deaf,
make your bodily eyes blind:
so shall you know the will of Christ and all the mystery of your salvation.
Saintly men and women, who rightly give glory to the Lord, give heed to the person within.
Our Lord, when he taught us
and set up a covenant for us
and formed us into his household, after he suffered, entered Sheol.

[101] 1 Tim 3.16.

He subjugated the entire earth,
and subjugated the nature of death to life.
When death saw him, ensouled, descending into Sheol, he mistakenly thought that this would be food for him, as was his wont.
Yet when he saw the splendor of the Godhead in him he called out with his voice saying:
"Who is this, clothed in the humanity that was subject to me, and has however conquered me?
Who is this who is wresting from destruction the flesh that was bound by me?
Who is this who is clothed in earth but who is yet of heaven?
Who is this born in corruption who is yet incorruptible?
Who is this stranger to my laws?
Who is this who is taking those who are mine?
Who is this who contends with the power of the flame of death and overcomes the darkness?
What is the new glory of this vision by which I am constrained from doing my will?
Who is this new dead one without sin?
Who is this who extinguishes darkness by the greatness of light, and will not let me govern those who are my own, but drags the souls that were given to me off to heaven?
What is this glory that keeps corruption from bodies?
Who is this whom I am unable to touch?
What is this glory inexplicable to those around it?
Woe to me! I am put to flight by him, and by those who are his, and have nothing with which to strike him."
This is the Christ who was crucified,
by whom whatever is on the left hand comes to be on the right,
and whatever was beneath is as that above,
and whatever was behind is as though in front.
When he rose from the dead,
and crushed Sheol,

and slew death with death, after he rose again on the third day,
he gave thanks to the Father, saying:
"I thank you, my Father, not with these lips that are fixed together,
nor with a bodily tongue, by which both truth and falsehood go forth,
nor with a word which derives from artfulness, and is thus material,
but I give thanks to you, King, with that voice that understands all things through you,
which issues from no bodily organ,
which falls on no fleshly ears,
which is not in the world,
which does not remain on the earth,
but with this voice,
the spirit that is in us, which speaks to you alone, Father,
loving you,
praising you,
through which the whole choir of perfected saints calls you beloved,
calls you Father,
calls you sustainer,
calls you helper,
since you are all, and all is in you.
Whatever is is yours, and nobody else's but only yours,
as you are to the ages of the ages. Amen."

Thus the shepherd should know the mysteries of every nature.

"After I have prayed to the Father," says Jesus, "I am taken up, as you know and as you see."

Thus it is right that the shepherd should give instruction in the presentation of the mysteries, so that they will be knowledgeable of whom they are partaking in the sacred things, and whose memorial it is they make in the Eucharist.[102]

[102] *Eucharistia* transliterated.

And afterwards, at the conclusion, he should say the following: "Since we have taken refuge in him also, learning that it is he only who gives, so let us beseech of him what he said that he would grant us, 'what eye has not seen, nor ear heard, nor human heart conceived, what God has prepared for those who love him,' as Moses and some other sainted men have said.[103] Since we have hoped in him let us glorify him, and to him be the glory and the power for the ages of the ages. Amen."

The people should say: "Amen."

After the people have been instructed in the presentation of the mysteries, the Eucharist[104] should be offered. But the presentation of the mysteries should not be pronounced on every occasion, but at the Pascha,[105] on Saturday, and on the first day of the week, and on the days of Epiphany and Pentecost.

29: What Kind of Person It Is Right for the Presbyter to Be A presbyter is ordained,[106] having been approved by all the people, in accordance with the statements that were made above.[107] He is to be capable in reading, humble, poor,[108] no lover of money, extensively ministering to the weak, tested, pure,[109] without blame, whether he is one who is like a father to orphans, whether he is one who ministers to the poor, whether he has not neglected the church,[110] in all things outstanding in devotion, gentle. Thus he may in all respects

[103]The most probable source of this citation is 1 Corinthians 2:9. Paul does not attribute it, and Origen plausibly suggests that it was derived from the *Apocalypse of Elijah* (*Commentary on Matthew* 27.9). Jerometraces it to Isaiah 64.3 (*Letter* 57.9).

[104]*Eucharistia* transliterated.

[105]*Pascha* transliterated.

[106]*Cheirotonētheis* transliterated.

[107]The Borgian Arabic adds "in the chapter regarding the appointment of a bishop."

[108]The Borgian Arabic reads "a lover of the poor," possibly correctly. The Ethiopic, however, supports the Syriac reading of "poor."

[109]Either "tested, pure" as here or "proved to be pure."

[110]This is the reading of the Borgian Syriac MS supported by Ethiopic. The other reads "if he has not grown cold for the church." Borgian Arabic reads: "If he has been diligent in attendance at church."

be worthy to have revealed to him by God whatever is fitting and whatever is suitable, and may also be found worthy of the gift of healing.

30 The appointment of the presbyter should be after this manner: as the entire company of priests leads him, and the bishop lays a hand on his head, as the presbyters touch him and hold him, the bishop begins to speak thus:

Prayer for the Ordination[111] *of a Presbyter*

"God, Father of our Lord Jesus Christ,
who are ineffable,
who are lustrous,
who have neither beginning nor end,
Lord, you have ordered all things and set them within a boundary,
and through reason have imposed order on all things created by you:
answer us, and look upon this your servant,
let him share in and grant him the spirit of grace, of reason, of fortitude,
the spirit of presbyterate, which does not grow old, which does not fail, of the same race,[112]
to love the faithful,
to admonish,
for the assistance and the governance of your people,
with labor, with fear, with a pure heart, with sanctity, and with prudence, and with wisdom, and by the operation of your Holy Spirit, through your concern, Lord,

[111] *Cheirotonia* transliterated.

[112] Possibly the earlier word is to be translated "indissoluble," and taken with this word (transliterating Greek *genos*), to refer to the relationship of the Spirit with the Father, thus indicating that the Spirit is inseparable from the Father's divinity, and is co-divine.

just as when you looked upon your chosen people, and commanded Moses to choose elders, and filled them with your Spirit, bestowing it on those who serve you,
so, Lord, pour out your unfailing Spirit that you gave to all who became your disciples,
and to all who, through them, have truly believed in you,
and make him worthy to be filled with your wisdom and with your hidden mysteries,
to shepherd your people with an upright heart, in purity and in truth,
while glorifying, while blessing, while praising, while giving thanks, while singing
hymns of glorification at all times, by day and by night, to your holy and glorious name,
while labouring with cheerfulness and patience to be a vessel of your Holy Spirit,
holding to, and carrying, at all times, the cross of your only begotten Son, our Lord Jesus Christ,
through whom, to you, be glory and might, with the Holy Spirit, unto all the ages of the ages."

And all the people should say: "Amen."

Then both the priests and the people give him peace with the holy kiss.

31 Thereafter he should be constant by the altar, laboring in prayer without ceasing. At home, on occasion, he may rest from the matters of the Lord's house, but should not cease or reduce praying for an hour.

He should fast three days throughout the entire year,[113] firstly so that he may be perfected in mind,[114] and again in accordance with

[113]That is to say, he is to fast for three days weekly, the same provision being made for the bishop, at 1.22 above.

[114]*Nous* is probably being rendered here.

his ability. So he should not be wandering around and moved by every wind, but laboring energetically in everything.

If it is revealed to a bishop or a presbyter that he should speak, he should speak. If not, then he should not neglect or disregard his work.

If it is revealed to a presbyter that he should visit his parishes[115] to speak the word, he should go. If it is not, he should call upon God in prayer. He should speak to them, if it is revealed that he should speak to them, bearing the load of the one who was crucified for him, carrying it at all times, and interceding for all the people.

A presbyter or a bishop should not be concerned about food or clothing. God has concern, and provides for those who are his, as he knows. If, when he has taken food or garment from one person, and it is said that he should receive some from another person too, it is enough that he take it from the first alone, and only as much as is fitting and necessary, and not excessively.

At all times the presbyter should be firm in the faith, and unchangeable, for such as these does God require. And he should examine the hearts of all so that no evil[116] within should be hidden or buried and alienate him from the grace of God.

He should not allow tares to grow in the good wheat, but should remove them, and should cut off those who introduce them. Darkness should not cover his light. He should constantly teach all the faithful to complete their course, as it were, in the day, as the children of light do not go around in darkness. The teaching of a presbyter should be appropriate, gentle, and measured, mingled with fear and trembling. The teaching of a bishop should be of the same strain. In teaching they should not speak vacuously, but should speak to their hearers what they may observe when they hear it. A presbyter should be mindful of all that he teaches, for in the day of the Lord a word of witness will be required of him of what he said to the people, so that those who

[115]The Syriac reads "strangers," which we may take as a misunderstanding of *paroikias*. Rahmani makes the correction.

[116]For "evil" (*byswt'*) the MSS read "in evil" (*bbyswt'*).

did not listen will be reproved. For he will stand before the glory of God, saying what he has taught. He should teach, then, so that he does not perish. He should pray for those who hear, that the Lord may grant them understanding of the Spirit, of knowledge, of truth.[117] Nor should they aimlessly throw pearls before swine, those who have heard and have labored, so that if the word has not borne fruit within them, but has perished, he may not provide the reason for its perishing. He should not give what is holy to the dogs,[118] but he should observe the indications of those who hear the word and bring forth good fruit. But he may leave all matters to the bishop without anxiety.[119]

He should not disregard or neglect those who, by means of teaching, perform good works. He should look out for these indications in them, making spiritual judgments concerning them: sighs, weeping, earnest discussion, silence, sadness, patience, bowing of the head.[120] But most effective in training and in causing grief is weeping and groaning. The work is vigils, continence, fasting, gentleness, prayer without ceasing, meditation, faith, humility, love for humanity, labor, worry, love, subjection, goodness, modesty, and all that is light. The indications of those who do not produce the fruit of life are thus: idleness, love of pleasure, eyes wandering to and fro, disobedience, complaining, fidgeting, inactivity, shiftiness. Their works are overeating, greed, anger, lack of faith, unsuitable and inappropriate laughter, carelessness, negligence, forgetfulness, discord, lewdness, love of gain, love of money, jealousy, contentiousness, drunkenness, haughtiness of mind, foolish talk, vaingloriousness, and all that is darkness.[121]

[117]Or perhaps, emending *swklʾ* to *swblʾ*, so reading "a share in the Spirit, in knowledge, in truth." The Ethiopic reflects a reading of "understanding of the Spirit of knowledge and truth."

[118]Mt 7.6.

[119]This sentence appears to be a gloss that has found its way into the text.

[120]Literally "in voluntary poverty of the head" or "ascesis of the head." Possibly intended to demonstrate humility, or perhaps an attitude of prayer. There is a detailed discussion in White, *Daily Prayer*, 96n279.

[121]We may, with White, *Daily Prayer*, 96–97, compare these lists of positive and negative qualities to those catalogued in Evagrius' *Praktikos*.

He should identify outcomes such as these, and address himself to those who are deserving. However he should not waste time with those who are not receptive of the word, for anyone who fruitlessly sows seeds into the ground shall reap misery.

The presbyter should go around to the houses of those who are sick with the deacon, as is right and proper, and visit them. He should consider what is fitting and useful to say to them, especially to the faithful. He should urge the church to assist those of the sick who are poor, so that those who serve with kindness may also enter into the joy of their Lord.[122] He should support those who have been taught recently[123] with statements from the prophets and the Gospels, with a word of instruction.

He should not neglect his own prayers, for he is the figure of the archangels; however, he should know that God did not spare the angels who sinned.[124]

He should fast. And he should receive of the cup if it is fitting. He should have as much wine[125] as, in his judgment, is suitable and helpful to him, so that the drink that is intended for his wellbeing is not taken for his undoing.

When in sickness he should eat herbs and fish, and again be concerned with his work. In all things the priest should be an example to the faithful in the work of holiness.

Let the presbyter praise and give thanks in the same way as the bishop.

32 Each of them should sing praise daily in the church, each at his own occasion.[126]

[122]Mt 25.21.

[123]I.e., new catechumens. The manuscripts read "disciplined."

[124]2 Pet 2.4.

[125]So the text. However if we were to read, as Cooper and Maclean, *Testament*, 188–189, suggest, *nsb mn ksʾ dhmrʾ* instead of *nsb mn ksʾ hmrʾ* (so the text), then that would mean: "He should receive as much wine from the cup as is fitting."

[126]Although this may mean "each at his own opportunity," White, *Daily Prayer*, 90, plausibly suggests that each might be allotted a time at which to pray. He points to Egyptian monastic *horaria*, which build on twelve daily synaxes, and links this to the provision of the *Testament* for twelve presbyters.

Daily Praise

"The grace of our Lord be with you."
The people: And with your spirit.
The priest: Glorify the Lord.
The people: It is right and just.
The priest: Your servants and your people glorify you,
incorruptible Father,
deliverer of our souls,
confirmer of thoughts,
guardian of our hearts:
you have illuminated our hearts and destroyed the darkness of our intellect by means of the knowledge that is within you.
You have restored to incorruption the old man, given over to corruption, by means of the cross of your only begotten one.
You have abolished error and brought humanity to immortality by means of your commandments,
and you have sought out the lost.

The people: We glorify you (and the rest).

The priest: We glorify you, Lord,
whom the archangels of unceasing praise glorify continuously,
and the glories of the glories,
and the chants of the principalities.
We glorify you, Lord who sent your intellect, your Word, your wisdom, your energy, the one who was with you of old, and was with you before the ages,
the uncreated Word from the uncreated one,
who appeared in flesh in the last days for the salvation of humanity that was made (by you),
your beloved Son Jesus Christ, so that he might set us free from the yoke of servitude.
On this account we, your servants, also glorify you as we are accustomed, and also your people:

The people: We glorify you (and the rest).

The priest: A threefold hymn of praise we sing to you from our hearts, Lord, giver of life.
You visit our lives of poverty,
you do not despise the spirits of those who are downtrodden,
the aid of those who are persecuted,
the helper of those who are tossed about on the sea,
the deliverance of those who are beaten down,
provider for those who are hungry,
revenger of those who are wronged,
lover of the faithful,
friend of the saints,
dwelling of the pure,
the habitation of those who call on you in truth,
protector of widows, liberator of orphans,
who have given your Church an upright constitution,
who have established in her love feasts,
ministries,
feasts for the faithful,
the fellowship of the Spirit,
gifts of grace and virtue.
We glorify you without ceasing at all times,
while contemplating in our hearts the image of your kingdom,
for your sake and for your beloved Son Jesus Christ,
through whom to you, with the Holy Spirit, be glory and power to the ages of the ages. Amen.

And the people should say: "Amen."

If anyone speaks prophetic utterances he should speak. He will have a reward.

In the middle of the night those of the priestly ministry, and those of the people who are more perfect, should sing praise individually. For it was at that hour that our Lord, when he arose, glorified his Father.[127]

[127]See 1.28 (part of the mystagogy) above. Note also the provisions for midnight

See, children of light, whoever believes in the words of the Lord conducts himself as he conducted himself in this world, in order to be where he is.

33: Regarding Deacons A deacon is appointed, having been chosen in accordance with what was said above (if he is of good conduct, if he is pure—if he is chosen on grounds of purity—and immune to distractions). Otherwise he is to be married to one wife, supported by all the people, not entangled in the affairs of the world, ignorant of any craft,[128] without riches or children. However, if he has a wife, or has children, his children should be instructed to perform acts of devotion,[129] and that they should be pure, and pleasing to the church in accordance with the law[130] of ministry. But the church should provide for them so that they can be constant in the law and in the work of ministry.

34 He shall be thoroughly engaged in the church, in whatever is right. His ministry is this: principally to do exclusively what is commanded of the bishop in communication.[131] He is to be adviser to the entire clergy[132] and the council[133] of the church. He is to minister to the sick, he is to minister to the stranger. He is to be the support

prayer in the *horaria* at 1.22 above and at 2.24 below, and in the provisions for widows at 1.42 below.

[128]The Borgian Arabic adds: "which would prevent him from works of religion."

[129]Following here the Paris MS. The other Syriac MSS have, "act nobly in fear." The correct reading *špyrwt dhltʾ* has become *špyrʾyt dhltʾ*. Rahmani makes the correction.

[130]*Kanōn* transliterated.

[131]An attempt to render *lsbrt*. Cooper and Maclean, *Testament*, 190, suggest emending to *lbdt*, thus reading the passage as "whatever is commanded of the bishop in ministry." This would conform it to *Apostolic Tradition*, and has much to commend it. The Ethiopic does not assist here.

[132]*Klēros* transliterated.

[133]Reading, with the MSS, (*rz*). Rahmani, *Testamentum*, 81, followed by Cooper and Maclean, *Testament*, 98, translates as "mystery," which is a possible meaning of the term. Cooper and Maclean suggest a confusion between *symboulos* (counsellor) and *symbolon* (symbol), but the suggestion is unnecessary.

of widows and a father to orphans. He is to go around all the houses of the needy in case there is anyone who is in distress, or sickness, or misery. He is to go around the houses of the catechumens, to confirm the doubting and to instruct the simple.[134] He is to clothe and make decent men who have died, he is to bury the strangers, he is to be a guide to those who travel from their homelands or who are in captivity. He is to make the church aware of those who are in distress so that they can be assisted.[135] He is not to trouble the bishop; however, on the first day of the week he is to mention everything, so that he is aware.

At the time of the assembly he should go around the church and be vigilant lest there is anybody there who is proud, or a joker, or a spy, or is talking foolishness. He should upbraid him in the sight and hearing of all, throwing out the one due punishment, to inspire fear in the others. If he persuades him to let him communicate, he should be comforted. If, however, the person continues in his offence, or his disorderly conduct, he should make a report concerning him to the bishop. He should be separated for seven days, and subsequently invited back, so that he is not taken captive. But if he persists, and continues in his folly when he comes back, he should be cut off until he truly repents, comes to his true self, and pleads (for admission).

If he is in a town at the shore of the sea he should walk around the areas at the shore occasionally lest there be anyone dead in the sea, whom he should dress and bury.

In the same way he should also search out the house of hospitality[136] lest anybody staying in that place is sick, or in need, or is dead, and he should make it known to the church so that what is right may be provided for each of them. He should bathe those who are paralyzed or infirm, as is right, so that they have some relief from their suffering. He should supply whatever is right for each of these by means of the church.

[134] *Idiōtēs* transliterated.

[135] So the Paris MS. The other Syriac MSS read "so that they can be remembered." (*wdrn*) has been miscopied as (*whrn*).

[136] The Paris MS has this in the plural.

Twelve presbyters, seven deacons, fourteen subdeacons, and three widows who sit in front are to be recognized in the church.[137]

From the deacons the one among them who is considered foremost in labor and in assistance is to be chosen for the reception of strangers. He should at all times be in the place in the church that is the house of hospitality, wearing white clothes with only a stole[138] on his shoulder.

35 In all things he is to be like the eye of the church. He is to be known with fear, to be an example of outstanding piety for the people.

He is to cry out thus:

The Deacon's Proclamation

"Let us arise.
Let each know his place.
Let catechumens depart.
Watch out for anyone polluted or idle.
Up with the eyes of your hearts.
Angels are looking on.
Anyone who does not trust should leave.
Let us beseech in a single mind.[139]
Nobody who is a fornicator, nobody who is wrathful.
Anybody who is a servant of wickedness should leave.
Watch out. We pray as children of light. We beseech our Lord, our God, our Savior Jesus Christ."

When the presbyter or bishop begins the prayer the people pray and bend the knee. After this the deacon speaks thus:

[137] Compare to this the provision of *Apostolic Church Order* for three widows and twelve presbyters. The Borgian Arabic reads: "There should not be more than twelve presbyters, seven deacons, four subdeacons and readers, three widows in a church, and singers to serve the priesthood."

[138] *Orarion* transliterated.

[139] Almost certainly rendering *homonoia*.

"Let us pray regarding the peace that is from heaven. That the Lord in his mercy may make peace for us.

Let us pray regarding faith. That the Lord may grant that our faith in him last until the end, and that he keep us in it.

Let us pray regarding harmony and singleness of mind, that the Lord may keep us in a single spirit.

Let us pray regarding patience, that the Lord may bestow patience until the end in all our adversities.

Let us pray regarding the apostles, that the Lord may grant us to be pleasing to him, as they were also pleasing to him, and that he may make us worthy of their inheritance.

Let us pray regarding the holy prophets, that the Lord may number us among them.

Let us pray regarding the holy confessors, that the Lord God may grant us completion with the same mind.

Let us pray regarding the bishop, that our Lord may grant us length of days in faith as he rightly shares the word of truth and presides over the church with purity and without blemish.

Let us pray regarding the presbyters, that the Lord does not remove from them the spirit of the presbyterate, bestowing on them diligence and outstanding piety until the end.

Let us pray regarding the deacons, that the Lord may grant them to run a perfect course, to attain sanctity, and to be remembered for their labor and their love.

Let us pray regarding the female presbyters, that the Lord may hear their intercessions, and guard their hearts with perfection in the grace of the spirit, and assist them in their labor.

Let us pray regarding the subdeacons, the readers, and the deaconesses, that the Lord grant them to receive their reward in patience.

Let us pray regarding the faithful laity, that the Lord grant them to keep the faith perfectly.

Let us pray regarding the catechumens, that the Lord grant them to attain the bath of regeneration, and sanctify them with the mark of sanctification.

Let us pray regarding the empire,[140] that the Lord may bestow peace on it.

Let us pray regarding the exalted powers, that the Lord may grant them understanding and fear of him.

Let us pray regarding the whole world, that the Lord may grant to each what is good for them.

Let us pray regarding those who sail and who travel by road, that the Lord may guide them with the right hand of mercy.

Let us pray regarding those who are persecuted, that the Lord may grant them patience and knowledge, and also bestow on them a completed task.

Let us pray regarding the departed who have fallen asleep in the Church, that the Lord may bestow on them a place of rest.[141]

Let us pray regarding those who have fallen away, that the Lord does not remember their folly and soften his rebuke upon them.[142]

Let us pray also regarding all of us who need prayer, that the Lord may protect us in a peaceful spirit, and guard us.

Let us persuade and pray the Lord to receive our prayers."

Then, after the deacon has made the commemoration the bishop shall sign with his hand and the deacon shall say: "Let us arise in the Holy Spirit, so that now that we have been made wise we may grow

[140]The Ethiopic reads: "for the emperor."

[141]After the petition for the departed, the Ethiopic has: "Let us pray regarding the suffering and the sick, that God may heal them quickly and send his mercy and sweetness to them."

[142]Ethiopic adds, after this petition: "Let us pray regarding rain, that the Lord may send rain on those places that need it. Let us pray regarding the fruits of the earth, that the Lord may give fruit to the earth from seedtime to harvest." There is no way of knowing whether these additional petitions have been inserted by Ethiopic or omitted by Syriac.

in his grace, while we glory in his name. Built on the foundation of the apostles[143] let us beg and pray to the Lord that he be moved to receive our prayers."

After this the bishop should complete, and the people should say "Amen."

36 The deacon should be like this: appearing to have fear, prudence, and reverence on account of the fervor of the Spirit. The conduct of his life should be perfect.[144]

He should examine and look at everyone who comes into the house of the sanctuary and should ask them where they come from, so that he can discern whether they are sheep or wolves. When he has inquired he should bring in anyone who is worthy, so that a spy might not enter and liberty of the church be investigated, and the fault should be upon his head.

If anyone comes late to worship, either when the dawn praise is being said, or when the sacrifice is being offered, whoever they are they should remain outside and the deacon should not bring them in, for it is a type of the day of judgment that is coming, in case the noise caused by the entrance should disturb those who are praying. However, when anyone comes and finds that the door is shut they should not knock, for the reasons stated above.

However, the faithful man or faithful woman should enter after the opening hymn of praise is finished, and the deacon should say "We make our supplication" either "over the offering" or "on account of the hymn of praise" "so that the Lord can write our supplication in the book of life and the God of the ages can bring us to his light-filled, sacred dwellings. Let us make our supplication for this brother who is late, that the Lord may grant him diligence, and labor, and

[143]Eph 2.20.

[144]Either as translated or: "appearing to have fear, prudence, and reverence. On account of the fervor of the Spirit the conduct of his life should be perfect" (so Rahmani, *Testamentum*, and Cooper and Maclean, *Testament*).

release him from every constraint of this world, and grant the desire for affection, and love and hope."[145]

After the same pattern also on behalf of a sister, or on behalf of a deaconess who comes late and remains outside. The deacon should make it known so that the entire people can intercede on their behalf. For when the deacon reminds people and makes it known with regard to them, there is an increase in diligence and a strengthening of the bonds of charity, and the careless and the idle are disciplined.

37 If there is a woman who suffers compulsion from a man, the deacon should investigate carefully, if she is faithful, whether she truly suffered compulsion, whether the man who practised compulsion was not her lover. And if all this is accurately (reported) and she that suffered is grieving over the compulsion that occurred, he is to bring this to the hearing of the bishop, so that she may be shown to be entirely in the communion of the Church.[146]

If the one who committed the compulsion is faithful, the deacon should not allow him into the church for communion,[147] even if he repent. If he is a catechumen, and repents, he is to be baptized and admitted to communion.

The deacon should catechize penitents, and should bring them to the presbyters or the bishop so that they may be catechized and taught knowledge.

If his competence is adequate[148] in ministering in the order of the diaconate he is to devote himself to prayer alone, and consider

[145]So the Paris MS and some Ethiopic MSS. The other Syriac MSS read "love in hope."

[146]Literally "a daughter of the church."

[147]"For communion" is supplied from the Paris MS. It is not in the other Syriac MSS, but is present in the Ethiopic.

[148]Rahmani, *Testamentum,* 91, suggests that "not" has fallen out here. The Borgian Arabic, which directs that the deacon, amidst his many duties, should not neglect prayer, supported by the Ethiopic, is perhaps the correct understanding of this provision.

intercession, meditation, love, the way, grief, as a work, fear before his eyes, and he is to be called a son of light.

38 The appointment of a deacon is thus: the bishop alone shall lay a hand on him, as he is not appointed to the priesthood but for the ministry of serving the bishop and the Church. The bishop shall speak over the deacon like this:

Prayer for the Ordination[149] *of a Deacon*

God who created all things, and adorned it by the word, who remain in realms of purity,
who through your servants the prophets have ministered to us eternal life,
who have enlightened us with the light of knowledge,
God, doer of mighty deeds and origin of glory,
Father of our Lord Jesus Christ, whom you sent to serve your will so that the whole human race might be redeemed,
and have made known to us and shown us your purpose, your wisdom, your energy, your beloved Son Jesus Christ,
the Lord of light, the leader of leaders and God of gods,
grant your spirit of grace and diligence on this your servant,
so that to him may be given diligence, gentleness, strength, and the power to please you.
Grant, Lord, that he may be a laborer in the law,
without disgrace,
kindly,
loving to orphans,
loving to those who are devout,
loving to widows,
fervent in spirit,
a lover of what is good,

[149] *Cheirotonia* transliterated.

and illuminate,[150] Lord, the one whom you have chosen and
elected for ministry in your Church,
offering with sanctity the offering to your sanctuary,
offered to you from the inheritance of your high priesthood,
so that ministering blamelessly, with purity and sanctity
and with a pure intention,
he may be found worthy of the high and exalted office through
your will,
praising you continuously through your only begotten Son Jesus
Christ, our Lord,
through whom, to you, be the glory and the power to the ages
of the ages.

The people: Amen.

39 If anyone bears witness and makes it known that he was in chains, imprisoned, or tortured on account of the name of God, a hand is not to be laid on him for the diaconate for this reason, in the same way not for the presbyterate, for the honor of the clergy[151] is his, since he was protected in his confession by the hand of God. However, if he is appointed as a bishop he is worthy of the imposition of a hand.

If he is a confessor who has not been judged by the powers, and not ill-treated in chains, but has simply confessed, he is worthy of the imposition of a hand; he receives the prayer of the clergy.[152] However he does not pray over him repeating all the words, but when the shepherd goes forward in promotion the effect is received.[153]

40: Regarding Widows A widow is appointed when she has been chosen, when she has remained unmarried for a long time, although

[150]Rahmani's text has "you have enlightened" (*wʾnhrtyhy*), a clear copying error for *wʾnhryhy*, as translated here.

[151]*Klēros* transliterated.

[152]*Klēros* transliterated.

[153]This final sentence is absent in the Borgian Arabic, though it may be a gloss. There is, nonetheless, something of this in Ethiopic, which is equally confused.

she has been pressed many times by people to marry, yet has not taken a husband on account of the faith. Otherwise it is not right that she should be chosen, but she should be tested for a time. Whether she is outstanding in devotion. Whether, if she has children, she has raised them in sanctity. Whether she has not instructed them with any worldly wisdom. Whether she has been a model for them of the sacred law and of the Church. Whether she has loved and honored strangers. Whether she has been constant in prayer. Whether she has lived humbly. Whether she has cheerfully relieved those in distress. Whether there has been revelation to the saints regarding her. Whether she has not neglected the saints. Whether she has ministered with all her ability. Whether she is able to bear and endure the burden.

She should be somebody who prays without ceasing, perfect in everything, fervent in spirit, the eyes of whose heart are open to everything, is constantly kind, loves simplicity, has no possession in this world but bears and carries round the cross at all times, who does evil to death, who day and night is assiduous by the altar, working cheerfully and secretly. If she has one or two or three of like mind in my name I am in their midst.[154] She should be perfect in the Lord, like one who is visited by the Spirit. Whatever is made known to her she should carry out with fear and diligence. She should exhort those women who are disobedient, she should instruct those women who are uninstructed, she should turn around those who are silly, directing them to modesty, she should test the deaconesses, she should inquire and determine of those women who come in of what sort they are, and who they are, and should admonish those who remain. She should patiently counsel female catechumens[155] in what is profitable; she should not speak to those who remain unpersuaded after three instructions. She should cherish those who desire virginity, or purity. She should admonish modestly and quietly those who oppose

[154]Clearly a reference to Mt 18.20, though something appears to be missing here. Cf. to this provision 1.22 above (regarding the bishop) and Ps.-Athanasius, *On Virginity* 10.

[155]Lit. "those (women) who hear."

themselves to her. She should be at peace with everyone. She should privately muzzle those who talk overmuch, and idly; if, however, they do not listen she should bring an old woman with her, or bring it to the hearing of the bishop. She should be silent in church.[156] She should be constant in prayer. She should visit women who are sick, and each Sunday she should take with her one deacon, or two, and assist them. If she has anything by way of possessions she should use them for the poor or the faithful. If she has nothing she should be assisted by the church. She should do no secular work, as though it were a trial to her; these, the works of the Spirit, should be hers: she should persevere in prayer and in fasting. She should not seek after profound matters. She should accept what the Lord supplies. She should not be anxious for her children, she should deliver them to the church so that they are fitted for the ministry of the priesthood by dwelling in the house of God. Her supplications before God will be acceptable; they will be the sacrifice and altar of God, for those who minister truly will be glorified by the archangels. As for those, however, who are licentious, and the intemperate, and drunkards, and gossips, and the curious, and the wicked, that is to say those who are lovers of pleasure, the images of their souls, set before the Father of light, will perish and be removed to the dwelling of darkness. For as their deeds, being visible, ascend on high they drag them, plainly, into the abyss so that, after this world is changed, and perishes, the images of their own souls will rise up against them, bearing witness, and will prevent them from looking up. For the image and likeness of every soul stands before God from the foundation of the world. For this reason the one who is able to approach the sacred vessels[157] is to be chosen. From these are the twelve elders who glorify my heavenly Father, they who receive the prayers of every pure soul, and offer the sweet odor on high.

[156]1 Tim 2.12.

[157]*Phialai* is transliterated and Rahmani, *Testamentum*, 97, suggested that the translator misread *phylai* (tribes) as *phialai* (phials). Thus the reference is one fit to meet the sanctified tribe. Cooper and Maclean find this unconvincing in view of the apparent reference here to Revelation 5.8.

41 Her appointment should be like this: while she is praying at the entrance to the altar[158] and looking downwards, the bishop, while the priests are listening, should say quietly:

Prayer for the Institution of Widows Who Are Seated Foremost

God, holy and exalted,
who look down on the humble,
who have chosen the gentle and the powerful,
who are honorable and created[159] the contemptible;
grant, Lord, your spirit of power to your servant, and strengthen her with your truth
so that, keeping your commandment and laboring in the house of your sanctuary,
she may be a vessel of honor for you, and may glorify you on the day when you, Lord, will glorify those who are poor for you.
Grant her the grace to fulfill with joy the instruction you have laid down as a rule[160] for your servant.
Grant her, Lord, the spirit of humility, of strength, of patience, of kindness, so that she may perform her tasks, bearing your yoke with ineffable joy.
Lord God, you really know our weakness;
perfect your servant in the glorification of your house,
empower her to be built up and a worthy example.[161]
Sanctify, give wisdom, give courage, God,
since your kingdom is glorious and blessed, God, Father,
and to you be glory, and to your only begotten Son our Lord Jesus Christ, and to the Spirit, holy, good, adorable, life-giving, consubstantial with you,[162]

[158]Or, following the Borgian Syriac, "at the eastern entrance." As observed in the notes to 1.19 above, the words are very similar.

[159]The Borgian Syriac has "called" (*qryt*) rather than "created" (*bryt*). This could well be correct. Ethiopic provides no guidance.

[160]*Kanōn* transliterated.

[161]*Typos* transliterated.

[162]If this doxology has not been interpolated, it is an interesting use of the recognition of the consubstantiality of the Spirit with the Father and Son at a relatively

now, before all the ages and for generations and to the ages.

The people: Amen.

42 Thereafter it should be thus. She should have no concern for anything, but should remain in solitude, to make supplications with greater piety and tranquility. For the foundation of sanctity and the life of a widow like this is solitude. For her affection is for none other but the God of gods and heavenly Father. She should give praise at the appointed times, by herself, during the night (and) at dawn. If she is menstruating she should remain in the temple and she should not approach the sanctuary. It is not as though she is polluted, but so that the sanctuary may receive honor. Afterwards, when she has fasted and bathed, she should be assiduous. But she should not fast during the days of the pentecost. On the feast of Pascha she should give of what she has to the poor, and bathe, and so let her pray.

When she is giving thanks or giving glory, if she has friends who are virgins, of like mind, it is good for them to pray with her, an account of the "Amen." But if not, alone, by herself, both in the church and at home, and especially in the middle of the night.[163]

The times at which she should give glory are the Sabbath and Sunday, either Pascha or Epiphany or Pentecost. The rest of the time she should offer thanksgiving in humility, with psalms, with hymns, with meditation, and so she should labor. So shall the most high sanctify them, shall forgive all the sins that previously were written down against them, and their error. My Father, the heavenly one, shall strengthen them and illuminate their countenances, like the countenances[164] of the holy ones that will shine with my glory on the day of retribution.

43 Her hymns of praise should be said thus, softly.

early stage. Cf. the language employed of the Spirit in relationship to the Father and Son in the presbyteral ordination prayer at 30 above.

[163]Possibly to be translated here as "at midnight."

[164]*Prosōpon* transliterated on both occasions here.

The Nocturnal Hymns of Praise of Widows

Holy, holy, spotless one, whose habitation is in the light,
God of Abraham and of Isaac, and of Jacob, God of Enoch and David, of Elijah, of Elisha, of Moses, of Joshua, and of the prophets and of the rest of those who proclaimed your name in truth,
God of the apostles,
who have guided all things by your reason and have blessed all who lovingly put their trust in you.
My soul glorifies you with all the power of my spirit,
my heart glorifies you, Lord, and your power at all times,
my whole ability glorifies you, Lord, because, if you so desire, I am yours, O God, God of the poor.
You are the helper of the lowly,
you look upon the humble and are the assistance of the weak.
Assist me, Lord,
since by your grace you have been pleased to make me your servant,
since you have granted me your great name, that I should be called a Christian.
You have set me free from servitude so that I may worship as a servant of God, powerful in eternity, and that I may glorify you, who look upon everything, without condemnation.
Confirm my heart in you, Lord God, until it is made perfect by the Holy Spirit.
Rejuvenate us for building up your holy Church,
Son and Word and thought of the Father,
Christ, who came for the salvation of the human race:
you suffered and were buried and you rose,
you were glorified again by him who sent you.
Turn to us and help us, Lord,
make our thoughts upright by the firm faith of the Spirit,

glorify your name in us since our hope into eternity is in your Father,
and in yourself, and in the Holy Spirit.

She should say "Amen" with those who are with her.

The hymn of praise at dawn, however, should be said thus:

Hymn of Praise, at Dawn, of the Widows Who Are Seated Foremost

God in eternity,
guide of our souls,
creator of light,
treasury of life,
delighting in the praises and prayers of the saints,
lover of mercy,
compassionate,
kind,
king of all things and God, our Lord,
my spirit glorifies you,
sending up the unceasing voices to you, of your servant, Lord,
who is beseeching you, that you may replenish in your servant the spirit of reason, devotion and of right knowledge.
I, Lord, give you glory:
you have removed from my poverty all trouble, disturbance, outrage,
and all contention and wicked habit.
It is you who have prepared and altered the senses of my mind[165] that I might serve you, God, alone,
you have adorned your holy Church with various ministries.
From your servant you drive away all doubt, fear, weakness, and direct the thoughts of those who rightly serve you.
I give you glory, God, who have illuminated me with the light of your knowledge
through your only begotten Son, our Lord Jesus Christ,

[165]White, *Daily Prayer*, 77–78, observes that this term seems to reflect an ascetic system similar to that espoused by Evagrius.

through whom be glory and power to you to the ages. Amen.

And she should say "Amen" with those who are with her.

44: Regarding Subdeacons[166] In this way a subdeacon is appointed, one who is devout,[167] the bishop praying over him. On the first day of the week, when all the people can hear, the bishop should say to him:

"You, *N*, serve and hear the gospel in the fear of God,
cultivate with piety the knowledge of your soul,
guard purity, be self-disciplined, be clean, and obey, and listen in humility,
and do not neglect prayer and fasting,
that the Lord may give you rest and make you worthy of a more exalted office."

And all the priests shall say: "Let it be, let it be, let it be."

45: On the Reader A reader is instituted, who is pure, gentle, humble, meek, wise, and highly experienced, learned, thoroughly instructed, of good memory, watchful, that he might also be considered for a more exalted office. Firstly a book is given to him, while the people look on, on the first day of the week. A hand is not laid on him, but he hears from the bishop: "You, *N*, whom Christ is calling as minister of his word, be careful and strive so that you appear tested in this rule,[168] and in a more exalted office also, by our Lord Jesus Christ, so that he may grant you a good reward on this account in his everlasting abodes." And the priest shall say: "Let it be, let it be, let it be."

46: On Male and Female Celibates[169] A male or a female celibate, however, is not instituted by any person, or appointed, but wills

[166] *Hypodiakonos* transliterated.

[167] Or "chaste."

[168] *Kanōn* transliterated.

[169] The Syriac has two words that are usually translated "virgin," first in the male form and secondly in the female.

to be set apart and adopts the title. Nor is a hand laid on anyone for virginity, for this arrangement[170] is the result of an individual's intention. It is right for a celibate to be fixed and bound in the wholehearted mortification of the body, to be constant in daily fasting and prayer, with weeping and grieving, at all times, however, expecting a departure from the flesh and striving as though at the departure. They should not cultivate raging, or greed, or drunkenness, or idle talk, or secular work, or distractions, but are to be like one who is on the cross. Their hearts are to be fixed on high, with complete humility of mind, and decoration,[171] with meditation on sacred books, with considerations of faithfulness, with thoughts[172] of kindness, so that when they pray they may be heard with regard to whatever matter they ask on behalf of the faithful who desire to provide for them. They should not reject, so that by means of them a portion of life should be shared out to them too.[173] They should be firm in love, and in kindness, and in constant and perfect goodness. They should be constant in consolations, consoling their neighbors. They should direct and instruct those who have recently been made members of the faithful, encouraging those who are very young with understanding, with knowledge and with kindness, being examples among them of sanctity in all good deeds.

[170]*Tagma* transliterated.

[171]So the text, reading *wmsbtwt*. However, the Ethiopic has "decorated with meditation," which may be the right reading. The Syriac would thus be, probably, *wmsbtyn*, of which the present text would be a plausible, though not obvious, corruption. Otherwise one might emend to *wswrtʾ*, which would mean "and character" here, though, once again, this is far from compelling.

[172]I have emended the Syriac here from *bwy* to *bwyn*, thus meaning thoughts or intention, rather than, as Rahmani's text, consolation. Ethiopic provides no guidance.

[173]So the MSS, with minor variations. The meaning seems to be that the celibates should not reject the offerings of the faithful laity, as by these offerings the donors may attain some portion of life. Lagarde repunctuates and reads the passage: ". . . they may be heard with regard to whatever matter they ask. They should not reject the faithful who desire to provide for them. . . ." This obviates the problem caused by the lack of an object for "reject," and so Cooper and Maclean, *Testament*, 113n11, find this possible. The meaning nonetheless remains that the faithful, through their support of the ascetics, may find some blessing.

Female celibates should act in the same way. They should speak and act with order,[174] with goodness and with knowledge, so that they will truly be the "salt of the earth," as they are called. But female celibates should cover their heads in church, concealing only their hair. They should be considered worthy of honor from all, so that the rest, who wish to, may be made envious of them.

47: Regarding a Charism If a person is perceived to have a spiritual gift of healing, or of knowledge, or of tongues, a hand is not to be laid on him, for the work is evident. They should, however, enjoy honor.

The first book of Clement is ended.

[174]*Taxis* transliterated.

2

The Second Book of Clement:

Commandments and Canons and Statutes That Our Lord Jesus Christ Established concerning the Order[1] of Those Who Are to Be Baptized[2]

1: Thus, regarding the Laity Those who come to hear the word for the first time, before they enter the congregation, are to be brought first to the teacher at the house. They are to be carefully examined so that their teachers may know why they have come, and what their desire is. And if they have come out of good intent, and are loving, they should be diligently instructed. Those who bring them should be advanced in years, faithful, known to the church. And they should bear witness as to whether they are fit to hear.

Inquiry should also be made regarding their conduct and way of life. Whether they are not contentious, whether they are gentle, whether they are humble, whether they are talkers of nonsense, or despisers, or lewd speakers, or jokers, or those who lead astray, or those who provoke laughter. Also whether any of them has a wife, or not, and if he has not, by his own intent, he should be patiently and diligently directed, and persuaded in a kindly manner to mend his ways. The bishop, moreover, shall take care of him in the Lord with prophetic statements that may lead him in the direction of purity. And if he makes progress, again with the teaching of the apostles, and afterwards with the Gospels, and with the perfect word of teaching, if he is worthy, he is baptized. And if he is worthy of the things

[1] *Taxis* transliterated.

[2] The title of Rahmani's text. That of the Synodicon text is more profuse.

that are hidden, he should hear these too, and so make progress in the things which are hidden.

If he desires to marry, that is no obstacle whatsoever; he shall avoid entrapment by the evil one with fornication. However, he should marry a faithful Christian woman, from the race of the Christians, who will be able to keep her husband in the faith. So should the bishop ordain, and take care that it is so.

Moreover, anyone who comes should be asked whether he is a slave or free, and if he is a slave whether he belongs to a faithful man, and if his master is allowing him to hear. And if his master is not faithful, and does not permit him, he should be persuaded to allow it. And if he says truly of him that he is coming to be a Christian out of hatred for his master the slave should be rejected. If no basis can be discerned that he hates being a slave, if he wishes to be a Christian, he should hear. If his master is faithful, and does not bear witness on his behalf, the slave should be rejected.

In the same manner also a man's wife should be instructed, as a wife, to be pleasing to her husband in the fear of God. If the two of them are desirous of cultivating purity on grounds of piety a reward is theirs.

Anyone who is not married should not commit fornication but should marry according to law. But if he wishes to remain so, he should continue in the Lord.[3]

If somebody is being troubled by a demon he should not hear the word from the instructor until he has been purified. For anyone who is constricted by a material spirit will be unable to receive the immaterial and sacred word. When he has been cleansed he may be taught in the word.

2 If anyone is a prostitute,[4] or a pimp,[5] or a drunkard, or a maker of idols, or a painter, or anyone from the theater, or a charioteer, or a

[3]Cf. 1 Cor 7.40.

[4]Or "female adulterer."

[5]Literally "somebody who provides for fornication." Possibly "a madam." Probably translating *pornoboskos*.

wrestler, or somebody who frequents the games,[6] or a gladiator, or a trainer of gladiators, or a state-employed hunter,[7] or a priest of idols, or a guardian of them, they should not be accepted. If anyone like this wishes to be one of the faithful they should desist from them, and when truly faithful,[8] and baptized, he should be accepted and communicate. And if he will not desist, he should be rejected. If anyone is a teacher of boys in worldly wisdom, it is better if he desist. However, if he has no other trade by which to make a living, he may be given allowance. If anyone is a soldier, in authority, he should be instructed not to be oppressive, not to kill and not to rob, not to rage and torture anyone, but to be content with the provisions that are supplied to him. But if they wish to be baptized in the Lord they are to desist from military service or from government. If not, they are not to be accepted. A catechumen, or one of the faithful, who desires to be a soldier should desist from this intention, or if not he should be rejected. For by his intention he has despised God, and left behind spiritual matters and perfected himself in the flesh and has treated the faith with contempt. If a prostitute, or a greedy man, or a drunkard do not continue in this way, and believe, and wish to become catechumens, they may. And if they make progress they should be baptized. If not, however, they should be rejected.

If a man's concubine is a servant, and wishes to be faithful, she may hear if she raises those who are born (of her) and separates from her master, or is joined to him in a single marriage. When she is baptized she may partake in the offering. If not, however, she should be rejected.

Somebody who does unspeakable things, or a diviner, or a sorcerer,[9] or a necromancer, should not come into consideration, as they are defiled. A spellcaster, or an astrologer, or an interpreter of dreams, or a soothsayer, or one who gathers together the people, or a stargazer, or somebody who divines by idols, should cease, and

[6]"Games": *agōn* transliterated.
[7]"State-employed": *dēmosion* transliterated.
[8]Or "when he acts faithfully."
[9]*Magos* transliterated.

be exorcized when he ceases and be baptized. If not, however, they should be rejected.

If a man has a concubine he should separate from her and marry in accordance with the law and should hear the word of catechesis.

3 Whoever has been taught with all care and hears the perfection of the gospel should be taught not less than three years. If he asks out of love to be baptized he should be baptized. If he is quiet, and humble, honest, and persevering, and remains with the one who is instructing him with labor, with vigils, with confession, in subjection and with prayer, and he desires to be baptized sooner, he should be baptized. For it is not time that is taken into account but desire of faith.

4 Those who have been taught should pray separately from the faithful after the instructor has finished, and depart, so the faithful may learn when the presbyter or the deacon reads from the New (Testament) or the Gospels.

The faithful women should stand in the church by themselves, and the female catechumens should be by themselves, separate from the female faithful, and they should all be separated from the men. The young girls should also be by themselves, each in accordance with order.[10] The men to the right and the women to the left. The faithful virgins should be in first place, and those who are being taught for virginity apart from them.

After the prayer the catechumens should give the peace to each other, the men to men and the women to women.

All the women should cover their head, together with their hair also. The women should adorn themselves properly and becomingly by showing modesty, not adorning themselves with plaited hair or stones,[11] so that the young men who are in the church are entrapped, but with modesty and knowledge. If not they should be taught by the

[10] *Taxis* transliterated.

[11] Cf. 1 Tim 2.9. This is a commonplace in the church order literature.

widows who are seated foremost, and if they resist in rebellion the bishop should upbraid them.

5 After the catechumens have prayed the bishop or presbyter should say the prayer of the laying on of the hand for catechumens while he lays a hand on them:

Prayer of Catechumens

"God, you send thunder and prepare lightning,
you fixed the heavens and founded the earth,
you enlighten the faithful and turn back those who are wandering,
you have given life to those who were dead, and given hope to those who were hopeless,
and you have freed the world from error through the descent of your only begotten Son Jesus Christ:
Answer us, Lord, and grant to these souls understanding, perfection, undoubting faith, knowledge of the truth, so that they may advance to a degree higher than this,
through your holy name, and through that of your beloved Son, Jesus, our Lord,
through whom be glory and power to you, with the Holy Spirit,
now and always and through all the ages of the ages. Amen."

And after this they should be dismissed.

If anyone, whilst a catechumen, is arrested for my name, and condemned to torture, and is in a hurry and pressing to receive the washing, the shepherd should not hesitate but should grant it to him. But if he suffers violence and is killed, without having received the washing, he should have no cause for anxiety, for he has been baptized in his own blood; he is justified.

6 However, if[12] each is chosen to receive the washing, they should first be examined and investigated, how they conducted themselves while catechumens,[13] whether they honoured widows, whether they visited the sick, whether they acted with all humility and charity, whether they were earnest in good deeds. Witness should be borne for them by those who brought them.

And every day that they hear the gospel a hand should be laid on them. They should be exorcized from the day on which they are chosen. And they should be baptized in the days of Pascha.

As the days draw near the bishop should exorcize each one of them by himself, so that he can be assured that each one of them is pure. If any of them is not pure, or if an unclean spirit is in any of them, they will be put to shame by that unclean spirit. And so, if anyone is found to be under such deception he should be taken away from among them, and reproved and blamed for not faithfully hearing the word of the precepts and instruction, because the wicked and alien spirit remained with him.

Those who are to receive the washing are to be instructed that they should wash and bathe their heads on the fifth day of the final week only. But if there is a woman who is then in the usual flux, she should wash and bathe beforehand again on a further day.

They should also fast, on the sixth day and on the Sabbath.

7 The bishop should gather together those who are receiving the washing on the Sabbath, and he should direct them to kneel while the deacon proclaims. And when there is silence he should lay a hand on them and say, as he exorcizes:

[12]So the text. However, one might expect "when" here both from the context and from the parallel in *Apostolic Tradition*. It is hard to account for the error either in Syriac or Greek.

[13]Or "while being instructed."

Exorcism before the Washing

God of heaven,
God of luminaries,
God of archangels who are subject to your authority,
God of angels who are subject to your power,
king of glories[14] and of dominions,
God of saints,
Father of our Lord Jesus Christ,
you have set free the souls that were enchained by death,
you have illuminated the one who was enchained in darkness
and fast-fixed by means of the fixing of the passion of your only begotten.
You have set us free from our bonds and have set us free from every weight that was on us,
you have repulsed from us every attack of the evil one.
Son and Word of God, you have made us immortal through your death,
you have glorified us with your glory,
you have set us free from the bands of our sins by your passion,
you have borne the curse of our sins by means of your cross,
and have taught us, humans, to become gods through your resurrection.
You have taken our humiliation on yourself and healed us[15]
and have trod for us the path to heaven,
and have transformed our corruption into incorruptibility.
Hear me, Lord, as I cry out to you in grief and fear.
Lord God, Father of our Lord Jesus Christ:
the one before whom stand the holy hosts of archangels and of cherubim and of armies without number, of principalities and seraphim.

[14]The Synodicon text reads "God of glories."

[15]"And healed us" is added following the Greek witness supported by the Synodicon text.

His veil is light, and fire is before his face.[16]
The throne of his glory is ineffable,
and the dwellings of delight that you have prepared for your saints[17] are ineffable;
their clothing and treasures are visible to you alone, and to your holy angels.
All things tremble before you and give you glory.
Your gaze measures the mountains and your name, when it is spoken, divides the depths.
The heavens, which are closed up by your hand, hide themselves from you,
the earth and the depths together tremble before you,
the sea and the dragons in it quake before you,
the wild animals[18] fear you with trembling,
the mountains and the firmament[19] of the earth melt with fear through you,
the winter storm quakes and trembles at your power,
and the raging whirlwind observes its limits.
On your account the fire of vengeance does not extend beyond the limit assigned, but shrinks back swiftly at your command.
On your account the whole creation is in travail, groaning with groans, under the order to wait until its time is due, from whom every opposing nature and creature flees.
On your account the entire army of the adversary is put down, the devil falls, the serpent is crushed and the dragon killed.
On your account the nations that confessed you are enlightened, and strengthened, Lord, by you.

[16]*Prosōpon* transliterated.

[17]So both Rahmani's text and the Ethiopic. The Greek witness has "those who love him," conforming the text to 1 Cor 2.9.

[18]The Syriac text has a singular here but the Greek witness is plural.

[19]The text has a plural here. The Greek witness is wanting here.

On your account is life revealed, hope is confirmed, faith is strengthened, and the gospel is proclaimed.
On your account is corruption brought to nothing and incorruptibility flourishes. Humanity was formed from earth by your hand, but is no longer earth when he believes in you.
Lord God omnipotent, I exorcize these in your name and (that) of your beloved Son, Jesus Christ. Expel from the souls of these your servants every disease and illness,
and every stumbling block and all unbelief,
all doubt and all contempt,
every unclean spirit working witchcraft,
that kills,
that is under the earth,
that is fiery, shadowy, foul-smelling, spell-binding, pleasure-seeking, gold-loving, arrogant, money-loving, angry.[20]
Now, Lord God,[21] annul within these your servants who have been named for you the weapons of the devil,
all sorcery,[22] magic, idol worship, divination, astrology, necromancy, stargazing, astronomy,[23] pleasure in the passions, wrongful lusts, grief, love of money, drunkenness, fornication, adultery, lasciviousness, rebelliousness, presumption, anger, confusion, wickedness, evil talk.
Now, Lord God, answer me, and breathe the spirit of calm on these your servants so that as they are guarded by you they may bring forth in you fruits of faith, of virtue, of wisdom, of purity, of self-discipline, of patience, of hope, of concord, of modesty, of praise.
Since by you have they been called as servants in the name of Jesus Christ,

[20]The Greek witness adds "promiscuous, every unclean demon, dark, formless, shameless."

[21]The Borgian Syriac and the Synodicon text read "My God."

[22]*Magyestēs* transliterated.

[23]The Greek witness adds "divination through birds."

being baptized in the Trinity,[24] in the name of the Father and of the Son and of the Holy Spirit,
witnessed by the angels, the glories, the dominions, all the heavenly host,
O Lord, the substrate of our lives and theirs, God,
guard their hearts,
since you are powerful and glorious to all the ages of the ages.

And all the people and the priests should say: "Amen. So be it, so be it, so be it."

If anyone gets up suddenly while the bishop is speaking, because he still has a possession,[25] and weeps or calls out, or foams, or gnashes his teeth, or stares, or is greatly disturbed, or runs away quickly and is seized, anyone like this should be put to one side by the deacons so that there is no disruption while the bishop is speaking.

Anyone like this should be exorcized by the priests until he is purified, and then he may be baptized.

After the priest exorcizes those who have approached (for baptism), or anyone who is found to be impure, the priest should breathe on them, and seal them between their eyes, on the nose, on the heart, on the ears. And so he should stand them up.

8 During the forty days of Pascha the people should remain in the temple, in vigil and prayer, hearing the Scriptures and praises, and words of teaching. On the final Sabbath they should rise early in the night, while the catechumens are being exorcized until the middle of the Sabbath night.[26] Those who are about to be baptized should not bring anything with them apart from one loaf for the Eucharist.[27] They should be baptized thus, when they come to the water. This water should be pure and flowing. First the infants, then the men, then the women. However, if any of those who approach wish to

[24]The Greek witness has "believing in the Trinity." Perhaps this is to be preferred, since the candidates are not actually baptized at this point.

[25]The Syriac is not altogether clear, but this seems to be the intent.

[26]Or, with a very minor emendation, "until the seventh hour of the night."

[27]*Eucharistia* transliterated.

commit to virginity, they should be baptized first at the hand of the bishop. The women, when they are baptized, should loosen their hair. All the children who are able to make the responses when they are being baptized should make the responses after the priest. However, if they are unable their parents should respond on their behalf, or somebody from their households. When those who are being baptized go down (to the water), after they have responded and spoken, the bishop should see lest[28] any of them, any man having a gold ring, or a woman having any gold (ornament) upon her person; for it is not right for anyone to have any alien object with them in the water. They should hand it over to those who are nearby.

When they are to receive the oil of anointing the bishop should pray over it and give thanks. And he should exorcise another with an exorcism such as that of catechumens. The deacon should hold that which has been exorcized and the presbyter should stand beside him. The one who stands beside that over which the thanksgiving for the oil has been said should be on the right, and the one who stands beside that which has been exorcized should be on the left.

As he takes hold of each of them he should ask, as the one being baptized turns towards the west, he should say: "I renounce you, Satan, and all your service, and your pomps,[29] and your pleasures, and all your works." And when he has said this, and made confession, he should be anointed with the oil that has been exorcized, while the one who anoints is speaking to him thus: "I anoint with this oil of exorcism for a deliverance from every evil and unclean spirit, and for a deliverance from all evil." And turning him to the east he should say:[30] "I submit to you, Father and Son and Holy

[28]This is the reading of the Paris MS; the others have "if." Perhaps this is a correction; it certainly makes more sense.

[29]Literally "your theaters."

[30]Rahmani, *Testamentum*, 128, suggests that there is something missing from the text and models this on the renunciation thus: "... he should say: 'Say: "I submit to you. . . ."'" This is plausible. Certainly we may accept that the candidate was prompted, as with the renunciation, and since a prompting is found in the Sahidic version (though this is independent). It is also possible that "turning him to the east" might, in the underlying Greek, be "turning himself to the east."

Spirit, before whom all nature trembles and is moved. Grant that I may blamelessly do your will."

After these things he should pass him over to the presbyter who is baptizing, and they should stand, naked, in the water, and the deacon should go down with him in the same way.

When the one being baptized goes down into the waters the one who baptizes should address him thus, while he places his hand on him: "Do you believe in God the almighty Father?" The one who is being baptized should say: "I believe." Straightaway he should baptize him the first time.

And again the priest should say: "Do you also believe in Christ Jesus the Son of God, who is of the Father, who from the beginning was with the Father, who was born from the Virgin Mary by the Holy Spirit, who was crucified in the days of Pontius Pilate, who died, who rose on the third day—he came to life from the dead and ascended into heaven and sat down at the right hand of the Father, and comes as judge for the living and for the dead?" When he says "I believe" he should baptize him a second time.

And he should also say: "Do you believe also in the Holy Spirit in the holy Church?" And the one being baptized should say "I believe." And so he should baptize him the third time.

Afterwards, when he comes up, he should be anointed by the presbyter with the oil over which the thanksgiving was said, while he says over him: "I anoint you with oil in the name of Jesus Christ." Women, however, should be anointed by the widows who are seated foremost, while the presbyter speaks over them. At baptism also these widows who are veiled should receive them under a veil, while the bishop says these professions. And thus also while he speaks to them of the things they are to renounce.[31]

[31] An emendation suggested by Rahmani, *Testamentum*, 130, is accepted here: the addition of the words "while he speaks." The apparent meaning is that widows are to anoint the female candidates before and after baptism and attend to them during the baptismal bath, while the bishop or presbyter says the prescribed words. Something is certainly wrong with the text as it stands, although the overall meaning is clear.

9 They should come together in the church, and after baptism the bishop should lay a hand on them, saying and invoking thus:

Invocation of the Holy Spirit:

"Lord God, through your beloved Son Jesus Christ you filled
your holy apostles with the Holy Spirit,
and through the Spirit allowed your blessed prophets to speak.
You have counted these your servants worthy, by means of your
oil,[32]
that they be counted worthy of the remission of sins by means
of the washing of rebirth,
and you have cleansed them of all the mist of error and
darkness of unbelief.
Make them worthy to be filled by your Holy Spirit, by the love
you bear for humanity,
while you bestow on them your grace so that they may truly
serve you according to your will, O God,
and may perform your commandments in sanctity and,
laboring at all times at whatever you desire,
may enter your everlasting habitations: through you, and
through your beloved Son Jesus Christ,
through whom, to you, be the glory and the power, with the
Holy Spirit to the ages of the ages."

In the same way, pouring the oil, placing a hand on his head, he should say:

"Anointing I anoint in God Almighty,
and in Jesus Christ,
and in the Holy Spirit,
that you may be a perfectly faithful servant to him,
and a vessel pleasing to him."

[32]So the MSS, reading *mšḥʾ*, though Rahmani, *Testamentum*, 130, emends to "by means of your Christ" (*mšyḥʾ*). The phrase may well be a gloss that has found its way into the text.

And as he signs him on his forehead he should give him the peace and say: "May the Lord God of the humble be with you." And the one who has been signed should respond and say: "And with your spirit." And so all of them, one by one.

10 And from then on they should pray together with all the people.

The offering should be brought up by the deacon, and the shepherd should give thanks. But the bread is offered as a type of my body. The cup should be mixed, being mixed with wine and water, for it is a sign of the blood and the washing, so that the inward person, that is related to the soul, should deserve what is like to it, and also, similarly, for the body.[33]

And all the people, in accordance with what was said above, should receive of the Eucharist[34] that is offered with "Amen." The deacons should hover,[35] as was said above. The one who gives should say "The Body of Jesus Christ, the Holy Spirit, for healing of soul and body." And the one who receives should say "Amen."

Whoever pours out from the cup is gathering judgment for his own soul. Likewise anyone who sees and is silent and does not reprove him, whoever he is.

Those who receive the offering should be exhorted by the priests to be constant in good works, to love strangers,[36] to labor in fasting, and in every good work. They are to strive in service.

[33]The meaning here is utterly obscure. Possibly it means that the mixed chalice feeds the soul in the same manner that the consecrated bread feeds the body. The Borgian Syriac manuscript seems to have attempted to tidy this up, only to make it further confusing.

[34]*Eucharistia* transliterated.

[35]It really is not clear what is meant. Rahmani, *Testamentum*, 133, suggests that this means that they wave fans. It may be that they are simply to "hover around"; it was said previously that the deacons should keep order, so this is perhaps what is meant; it is also possible that this was the original meaning, and that Jacob had misunderstood a word like *perikeimai*.

[36]Heb 13.2.

They are also to be taught regarding the resurrection of the body, for nobody should know the teaching concerning the resurrection before they are baptized. For this is the new statute,[37] which has a new name, which nobody knows apart from those who receive.

A deacon does not give the offering to a presbyter. He should uncover the disc[38] or paten, and the presbyter should receive (it).[39]

The deacon should give to the people with his hand.[40]

When the presbyter is not present the deacon, if necessary, should baptize.[41]

11 If anyone receives a ministry to carry to a widow or to a poor woman or to any one constantly engaged in the business of the Church he should give it on the same day; when it is the following day, he should add something to it from his own goods, and give it then. For the bread of the poor was with him.

The bread and the cup should be offered in the last week of Pascha, on the fifth day of the week. And the one who suffers on behalf of what he offers is the one who approaches.[42]

[37]Syriac *psq*). This is an alternative rendering of the Greek *psēphos* (stone), which certainly stood in the Greek. The translator, Jacob, apparently did not recognize the reference to Rev 2.17.

[38]*Pinax* transliterated.

[39]See my "The Deacon's 'Garment' at *Traditio Apostolica* 22: An Attempt at Understanding," *St Vladimir's Theological Quarterly* 61 (2017): 119–122, for a retrojection of the Greek of *Apostolic Tradition* and its meaning. The custom described in *Apostolic Tradition*, namely the carrying of bread from the bishop's altar to the presbyters of the city, a practice known as the *fermentum*, would be entirely unfamiliar to Jacob, the translator, and so he seeks to recast it in an attempt to make sense of it.

[40]Cooper and Maclean (*Testament*, 129) construe this as into his (that is the people's) hand(s). They comment that the rendition as given above does not make sense. However, the redactor, not the translator here, is trying to make sense of a somewhat oblique part of *Apostolic Tradition* in which the *fermentum*, unknown outside Rome, is being described. Thus he turns it into a description of the administration of communion in a church. The point is that when giving communion to a presbyter it is suggested that the deacon should give the vessel to the presbyter so that the presbyter can communicate himself, but that in giving communion to the people he should give it directly (with his own hand).

[41]The Borgian Syriac omits this sentence.

[42]Such is the literal translation of the MSS. It is hard to make any sense here.

The lamp should be offered in the temple by the deacon, as he says: "The grace of the Lord be with you all." And all the people should say: "And with your spirit."

The little boys should sing spiritual psalms and hymns of praise by the light of the lamp. All the people, all together, their voices in harmony, should respond to the psalm and to the song, "Alleluia." Nobody should kneel until the one who is speaking has ceased. In the same way, also, when a reading is read or a word of instruction is spoken. If the name of the Lord is thus uttered, and the rest, as has already been adequately discussed, nobody should bow, coming in creeping.[43]

12 The conclusion of Pascha is at midnight following the Sabbath. During the fifty days nobody should fast or bend the knee, for these are days of quietness and gladness. Those who bear the burdens of labor should refresh themselves a little during the fifty days, and on every first day of the week.

Before offering the offering the bishop should say what is appropriate for the offering while those who are clothed in white should receive from each other and say "Alleluia."

13 At a supper or a meal, those who have come together should receive from the shepherd thus, as for a blessing. A catechumen should not receive.

Anyone who is of the household, or a family member, of somebody who is a pagan teacher[44] should not associate with him, should not give praise with him, nor should he eat with him on account of family relationship or on account of being agreeable, in case he

Possibly *dhš hlp hw* might be emended to *dhšh lw hw* and rendered as "the one who is worthy of him, him who made the offering, (namely Christ), should approach." The Borgian-Arabic and the Ethiopic completely recast the passage.

[43]Cooper and Maclean, *Testament*, 130, reasonably annotate "Meaning?" They add: "Perhaps *private* devotions are forbidden during *public* service." White, *Daily Prayer*, 150, suggests that it means that nobody who is an interloper (thus coming creeping in) should participate in the liturgy (that is, bow). This seems more likely.

[44]Literally "one who teaches otherness."

reveal something that is not to be said to a wolf, and so come under judgment.

Those who are invited, with the bishop, to the house of one of the faithful, should eat with moderation and knowledge, and not with drunkenness or gluttony, not to make anyone nearby laugh, and not to cause annoyance to the household of whoever invited them. They should enter in such a way that the one who invited them should give thanks that the saints are entering his house.[45] For you have heard that you are the salt of the earth,[46] because when they eat they will eat abundantly so that there may be (food) left over for yourselves, and also for those to whom the one who invited you wants to send, who may have them as foodstuffs left by the saints and may rejoice at what remains.

Those who are invited to a feast should not stretch out a hand before those who are elder, but the last should eat when[47] the first be finished.

Those who eat should not be uproarious[48] when speaking, but they should eat in silence. But if somebody wants something, or the bishop or presbyter asks, he should render an answer. Yet when the bishop says something, everybody, praising quietly, should be silent unless he is also asked a question.

14 If anyone should bring fruits, or the first produce of crops, as first fruits, he should offer them to the bishop.[49]

15 If anybody who has children departs from the world, whether a faithful man or a faithful woman, they should give their goods to the church so that the church may provide for their children and give

[45]Or "pray that the saints may enter his house."

[46]Mt 5.13.

[47]Literally, "and."

[48]Reading (and interpreting) *ntktswn*. The Paris MS has "take offense" (*ntkslwn*).

[49]Or, with some repunctuation, "If anyone should bring fruits, or the first produce of crops, he should offer them to the bishop as first fruits."

relief to the poor from what is theirs, so that God may grant kindness to their children and rest to those who have fallen asleep.[50]

Somebody who has no children should not have many goods, but he should give the greater part of his goods to the poor and to the imprisoned.[51] He should retain for himself only whatever is right and sufficient. If somebody has goods[52] and desires to discipline himself in virginity, he should give all his goods to the poor and discipline himself, and remain in the church, persevering in prayer and thanksgiving.

16 The bishop should bless thus the fruits that are offered to him:

"We give you thanks, O God, at all times, and also on this day when we offer you the firstlings of the fruits that you have given us for food.
You have brought them to fruition by your power and by your word, commanding at the beginning of the creation of the worlds that the earth should bring forth various fruits for the enjoyment and pleasure of humanity and all animals.
We give you glory, Lord, for all these things with which you have cared for us, adoring all the earth for us with assorted fruits.
Bless also this your servant, *N*, and receive his diligence and his love,
through your beloved Son, Jesus Christ, through whom to you be glory, honor, and praise with the Holy Spirit to all the ages of the ages. Amen."

[50]Here following the Paris MS and the Synodicon text in reading "rest to those who have fallen asleep" (*dskbw*) instead of "rest to those who have left (them) behind" (*dsbqw*) (so the other Syriac MSS). The reading is adopted as the MSS that contain it are of far greater antiquity, and because the absence of any object to the verb in the other MSS is problematic. This reading, moreover, has support from the Ethiopic.

[51]Lit. "prison."

[52]Reading "goods" (*qnyn'*) with the Paris MS and the Synodicon text, supported by Ethiopic, instead of the "children" (*bny'*) of the other Syriac MSS. That text would stand in contradiction to the Canon 15 of Gangra, forbidding persons to neglect their children under the excuse of asceticism.

Vegetables are not blessed but fruits of trees; flowers both rose and lily.

17 In everything that they take and eat, the faithful should praise and give thanks, and should eat without scandal or scruple. A person should not taste of anything which is strangled or which has been offered to idols.[53]

18 On the days of Pascha, particularly on the final days, the Friday and the Saturday, prayers, with the corresponding number of canticles, should be said night and day. The word should be expounded extensively, and the readings should be various and continuous. The vigils and the anticipations of the night should be seemly.

19: Regarding the Deacons Who Go out and Pass among the Women in Case There Are Infants Who Are Not in Order The readers should assist them; in the same way the subdeacons also. They should not allow them to sleep, for that very night is a figure of the kingdom, and especially that of the Sabbath.

Those who labor and toil should toil until midnight.

The catechumens should be dismissed first, when they receive blessings from the broken loaf.

The faithful, when they are dismissed, should depart in order and knowledge to their homes. They should not be forgetful of the prayers in their feasts.

The priests should not break off from their administrations.

The women should depart, each accompanying her husband.

The widows should remain in the temple until dawn, having food there.

The virgins should remain in the temple together, and the bishop should help them and provide for them; and the deacons should minister to them.

[53] Acts 15.29. This provision continues to appear in the church order literature and in conciliar canons.

The older women should remain with the bishop until dawn, while they pray and rest. In the same way also those who are newly baptized.

The girls who are ready for marriage should depart accompanying their mothers. Such is fitting.

20 The bishop should command them to proclaim that no one is to taste of anything until the offering is completed. And the whole body of the church shall receive a new food. Afterwards, in the evening, those who are to be baptized are to be baptized, after one reading.

If any person eats something else before he approaches and receives of the Eucharist he has sinned, and his fast is not credited to him.

A hand is laid on the catechumens when they are dismissed.

If anyone of the faithful remains at home through illness the deacon should carry the offering to him.

If there is any presbyter[54] who is unable to attend, a presbyter should carry it to him.

In the same way, if a woman is pregnant and sick[55] and unable to fast for these two days she should fast this one day, while taking bread and water on the first day. And if she is unable to attend, a deaconess should carry it to her.

21: Regarding the Sick They should bring this to the attention of the bishop, so that, if it seems good to the bishop he might visit them. For the sick person is greatly comforted, especially if he is faithful, when the chief of the priests remembers him.

22 In the church, the virgins and the boys should sing in response to the psalm-singer. However, if they are singing psalms privately, at home, two or three of them, they should respond to one another

[54]The construction here makes it possible that an elderly man is intended.
[55]The Paris MS and the Synodicon text simply have "pregnant."

when they sing the psalms. In the same manner, the men should also act thus.

23 If a poor person dies those who make provision for all such needs should be responsible for his clothing.

If a stranger dies those who have a space should grant it. But if the church has one it should give it. And if he has no covering the church should grant it in the same way. If he does not have the means for burial, he should be buried.[56]

If a person is found to have had possessions, and he does not leave them to the church, they should be retained for a period. After a year the church should not appropriate them but they should be given to the poor, for his soul.

If he wishes to be embalmed the deacons should undertake this in the presence of a presbyter.

If the church is in possession of a graveyard and there is somebody who remains there and keeps it, the bishop should make provision for him from the church so that he is not a burden on those who visit it.

24 At all times the people should be observant of the earliest dawning. They should pray as soon as they have gotten up and washed their hands. Then each should go to the work he desires.

Everyone should be observant of prayer at the third hour, with grieving and labor,[57] either in the church or in the house since they cannot attend. For this is the hour of the fixing to the cross of the only begotten.

[56]The intent, as Rahmani, *Testamentum*, 143, notes in a parenthetical addition to his translation, is that the church should make itself responsible for the burial of strangers and paupers. However, this last sentence might be translated (so Cooper and Maclean, *Testament*, 135) as "if he has no grave-clothes, he should be shrouded," the word for "shrouding" and "burial" being the same.

[57]Cf. the provisions of Ps.-Athanasius, *On Virginity* 12 (regarding the sixth hour) that prayer be accompanied by "grieving and begging."

Likewise at the sixth hour there should be prayer with sorrow, for then the daylight was divided by the darkness. Then there should be a voice like that of the prophets and of creation grieving.

Again at the ninth hour there should be extended prayer, with glorification, like the souls of those who glorify God, who is without deceit, who remembers his holy ones and who sent his Word and wisdom to enlighten them. For at this hour life was opened to the faithful, and blood and water were poured forth from the side of our Lord.

At evening, which is the onset of another day, demonstrating a likeness of the resurrection, he has given us cause for glorification.

At midnight they should get up with glorification and with extolling, on account of the resurrection.[58]

At dawn glorification with psalms, because after he arose he glorified the Father while they were singing psalms. However, if anyone has a consort[59] or a wife who is faithful,[60] the husband who is faithful should of necessity go and pray at these times.

Those who are chaste should not reduce anything. For the ornaments of heaven, the luminaries, the sun, the moon, the stars, the lightnings, the thunders, the clouds, the angels, the archangels, the glories, the dominions, the whole host, the depths, the sea, the rivers, the springs, fire, dew, and all nature that produces rain give glory. All the saints, and all the souls of the just, also give glory. Thus those who pray are numbered together in the remembrance of God.

25 When you complete these matters, you who are faithful, instruct and admonish one another, when you ensure that the catechumens

[58]Cf. Ps.-Athanasius, *On Virginity* 20: "Get up at midnight and hymn the Lord your God. For at that hour our Lord rose from the dead and hymned the Father."

[59]The suggestion of Cooper and Maclean, *Testament*, 136. The Syriac reads, literally, "daughter of the partaking of marriage."

[60]Rahmani, *Testamentum*, 144–145, suggests that the Borgian Arabic should be followed, which reads: "who is not faithful." That would conform to the wider witness to *Apostolic Tradition*, from which this is ultimately derived, though it is also possible that the translator was confused, or attempting to introduce some form of correction. The Ethiopic reads as the Syriac, thus omitting the negative.

progress, when you are loving to all, you will not perish but will be in me, and I will be among you.

The faithful should always be careful to partake of the Eucharist[61] before eating, so as to be incapable of receiving any harm.

When you teach these matters and observe them you shall be redeemed and the wickedness of heresy[62] shall not prevail against you.

Thus I have now taught you all that you desire, what I spoke with you about from the beginning, and so you know what I have taught and commanded you before I suffer.

26 And especially you, John and Andrew and Peter, know now everything that I spoke to you while I was with you, as also what is in this Testament, so that when you deliver it to the nations the will of my Father may be accomplished at all times, as you remain firm in preserving it, so may there be good fruits in those who hear it.

You know from what I have told you that a good tree cannot produce bad fruit.[63] So do everything that I have commanded you, both openly and secretly. And the God of peace be with you."

27 Then we fell down and worshipped him saying: "Glory to you, Jesus, name of light, who gave us the teaching of your commandments so that we, and all those who hear you, could be like you." When he spoke to us, taught and commanded us, and he showed us many healings[64] and works of power, he was taken up from us, giving us tranquillity.

John and Peter and Matthew wrote this Testament and sent copies from Jerusalem by the hands of Dositheus and Silas and Magnus and Aquila,[65] whom they chose as those sent to every inhabited place. Amen.

[61] *Eucharistia* transliterated.
[62] *Hairesis* transliterated.
[63] Mt 7.18.
[64] Literally "loosings."
[65] Although we may venture identities for these names, this can be little more

The second book of Clement is concluded, translated from the language of the Greeks into Syriac by Jacob the poor[66] in the year 998 of the Greeks.[67]

than speculation. It is hard to see a rationale behind the choice of these obscure figures as carriers of the *Testament*.

[66]Jacob (or James) was a bishop in Edessa in the latter part of the seventh and early part of the eighth centuries, though due to political troubles he spent the greater part of his life in different monasteries. He was a prolific author, biblical commentator, canonist, grammarian, translator, and historian.

[67]686/7. The colophon (conclusion) of Rahmani's text. The Synodicon text simply has "The Testament ends here."

Bibliography

1: Textual materials for the study of the *Testament*, and translations

Arendzen, J. P. "A New Syriac Text of the Apocalyptic Part of the 'Testament of the Lord.'" *Journal of Theological Studies* 2 (1901): 401–416.

Beylot, Roger. *Testamentum Domini éthiopien: Édition et traduction.* Leuven: Peeters, 1984.

Burmeister, Otto. "The Coptic and Arabic Versions of the Mystagogia." *Le Muséon* 46 (1933): 203–235.

Chronz, T., and H. Brakmann. "Fragmente des Testamentum Domini in georgischer Übersetzung." *Zeitschrift für antikes Chistentum* 13 (2009): 395–402.

Cooper, James, and Arthur J. Maclean. *The Testament of Our Lord.* Edinburgh: T&T Clark, 1902.

Corcoran, Simon, and Benet Salway. "A Newly Identified Greek Fragment of the *Testamentum Domini.*" *Journal of Theological Studies* 62 (2011): 118–135.

Gain, B. "Fragments grecs inédits du Testamentum Domini attribués à Saint Basile." *Augustinianum* 32 (1992): 261–277.

Kohlbacher, Michael. "Georgische Paralleltexte zum *Testament unseres Herrn Jesus Christus* (CPG 1743)." In *Akten des 5. Symposiums zur Sprache, Geschichte, Theologie und Gegenwartslage der syrischen Kirchen (V. Deutsche Syrologentagung) Berlin 14.–15. Juli 2006*, edited by Rainer M. Voigt, 97–126. Aachen: Shaker, 2010.

Lagarde, Paul de. *Reliquiae iuris ecclesiastici antiquissimae, graece et syriace.* Leipzig: Teubner, 1856.

Nau, F. "Fragment inedit d'une traduction syriaque jusqu'ici inconnue du Testamentum D.N. Jesu Christi." *Journal Asiatique* 17 (1901): 233–256.

Rahmani, Ignatius Ephraem II. *Testamentum Domini nostri Jesu Christi.* Mainz: Kirchheim, 1899.

Sperry-White, Grant. *The Testamentum Domini: A Text for Students, with Introduction, Translation, and Notes.* Bramcote: Grove, 1991.

Troupeau, Gérard. "Une version arabe de l'anaphore du *Testamentum Domini.*" In *Christianisme oriental: kérygme et histoire; mélanges offerts au père Michel Hayek,* edited by Charles Chartouni, 247–256. Paris: Librairie orientaliste Paul Geuthner, 2007.

Vööbus, Arthur. *The Synodicon in the West Syrian Tradition.* 2 vols. in 4 pts. Corpus Scriptorum Christianorum Orientalium 367–378, 375–376. Leuven: Peeters, 1975–76.

2: Studies of the *Testament* and works substantially discussing the *Testament*

Arranz, Miguel. "Les rôles dans l'assemblée chrétienne d'après le 'Testamentum Domini.'" In *L'Assemblée liturgique et les différents roles dans l'Assemblée,* 43–77. Rome: Edizioni liturgiche, 1977.

Baumstark, Anton. "Die arabischen Texte der *Diathēkē tou Kuriou.*" *Römische Quartalschrift* 14 (1900): 291–300.

Bleckmann, Bruno. "Apokalypse und kosmische Katastrophen: das Bild der theodosianischen Dynastie beim Kirchenhistoriker Philostorg." In *Endzeiten: Eschatologie in den monotheistischen Weltreligionen,* edited by Wolfram Brandes and Felicitas Schmieder, 13–40. Berlin: de Gruyter, 2008.

Botte, Bernard. "L'epiclèse de l'anaphore d'Hippolyte." *Recherches de Théologie Ancienne et Médiévale* 14 (1947): 241–251.

Bouyer, Louis. *Eucharist: Theology and Spirituality of the Eucharistic Prayer.* Notre Dame: University of Notre Dame, 1968.

Connolly, R. H. *The So-Called Egyptian Church Order and Derived Documents.* Cambridge: Cambridge University Press, 1916.

Coquin, René-Georges. "Le Testamentum Domini: problèmes de tradition textuelle." *Parole de l'Orient* 5 (1974): 165–188.

Funk, F. X. *Das Testament des Herrn and die verwandten Schriften.* Mainz: Kirchheim, 1901.

Kohlbacher, Michael. "Das Kirchenbau-Kapitel des Testamentum Domini Nostri Jesu Christi." In *Architektur und Liturgie: Akten des Kolloquiums vom 25. bis 27. Juli 2003 in Greifswald,* edited by Michael Altripp and Claudia Nauerth, 35–38. Wiesbaden: Ludwig Reichert, 2006.

______. "Wessen Kirche ordnete das *Testamentum Domini Nostri Jesu Christi?* Anmerkungen zum historischen Kontext von CPG 1743." In *Zu Geschichte, Theologie, Liturgie und Gegenwartslage der syrischen Kirchen*, edited by Martin Tamcke and Andreas Heinz, 55–137. Münster: Lit, 2000.

Ligier, Louis. "L'anaphore de la 'Tradition apostolique' dans le Testamentum Domini." In *The Sacrifice of Praise: Studies on the Themes of Thanksgiving and Redemption in the Central Prayers of the Eucharistic and Baptismal Liturgies in Honour of Arthur Hubert Couratin*, edited by B. D. Spinks, 91–106. Ephemerides liturgicae, Subsidia 19. Rome: Edizioni Liturgiche, 1981.

Morin, G. "Le Testament du Seigneur." *Revue Bénédictine* 17 (1900): 10–28.

Pallas, Dimitrios. "L'édifice cultuel chrétien et la liturgie dans l'Illyricum oriental." In *Eisēgēseis tou Dekatou Diethnous Sunedriou Christianikēs Archaiologoias*, 497–570. Thessaloniki: Société d'études macédoniennes, 1980.

Parisot, Jean. "Note sur la mystagogie du 'Testament du Seigneur.'" *Journal asiatique* 9.15 (1900): 377–380.

Post, Paul. "La liturgie en tant qu'architecture?" *Bijdragen* 42 (1981): 392–420.

Quasten, Johannes. "Die Ostervigil im Testamentum Domini." In *Paschatis sollemnia: Studien zu Osterfeier und Osterfrömmigkeit*, edited by Balthasar Fischer and Johannes Wagner, 87–95. Basel: Herder, 1959.

Richardson, C. C. "A Note on the Epicleses in Hippolytus and the Testamentum Domini." *Recherches de Théologie Ancienne et Médiévale* 15 (1948): 357–359.

Schwartz, E. *Über die pseudapostolischen Kirchenordnungen.* Schriften der wissenschaftlichen Gesellschaft im Strassburg 6. Strassburg: Trübner, 1910.

Sperry-White, Grant. "The Imagery of Angelic Praise and Heavenly Topography in the *Testament of Our Lord.*" *Ecclesia orans* 19 (2002): 315–332.

Steimer, Bruno. *Vertex traditionis: Die Gattung der altchristlichen Kirchenordnungen.* Berlin: de Gruyter, 1992.

Stewart, Alistair C. "The Deacon's 'Garment' at *Traditio Apostolica* 22: An Attempt at Understanding." *St Vladimir's Theological Quarterly* 61 (2017): 119–122.

______, "The Apocalyptic Section of *Testamentum Domini*: An Attempt at Dating." *Journal of Theological Studies* 62 (2011): 136–143.

White, Grant. *Daily Prayer and Its Ascetic Context in the Syriac and Ethiopic* Testamentum Domini. Joensuu: University of Joensuu, 2002.

Wordsworth, J. "The 'Testament of Our Lord.' Part II: Its Connexion with the School of Apollinarius of Laodicea." *Church Quarterly Review* 99 (1900): 1–29.

POPULAR PATRISTICS SERIES

1 *On the Priesthood* – St John Chrysostom
4 *On the Divine Images* – St John of Damascus
6 *On the Holy Icons* – St Theodore the Studite
7 *On Marriage and Family Life* – St John Chrysostom
8 *On the Divine Liturgy* – St Germanus
9 *On Wealth and Poverty* – St John Chrysostom
10 *Hymns on Paradise* – St Ephrem the Syrian
11 *On Ascetical Life* – St Isaac of Nineveh
12 *On the Soul and Resurrection* – St Gegory of Nyssa
13 *On the Unity of Christ* – St Cyril of Alexandria
14 *On the Mystical Life*, vol. 1 – St Symeon the New Theologian
15 *On the Mystical Life*, vol. 2 – St Symeon the New Theologian
16 *On the Mystical Life*, vol. 3 – St Symeon the New Theologian
17 *On the Apostolic Preaching* – St Irenaeus
18 *On the Dormition* – Early Patristic Homilies
19 *On the Mother of God* – Jacob of Serug
21 *On God and Man* – Theological Poetry of St Gregory of Nazianzus
23 *On God and Christ* – St Gregory of Nazianzus
24 *Three Treatises on the Divine Images* – St John of Damascus
25 *On the Cosmic Mystery of Christ* – St Maximus the Confessor
26 *Letters from the Desert* – Barsanuphius and John
27 *Four Desert Fathers* – Coptic Texts
28 *Saint Macarius the Spiritbearer* – Coptic Texts
29 *On the Lord's Prayer* – Tertullian, Cyprian, Origen
30 *On the Human Condition* – St Basil the Great
31 *The Cult of the Saints* – St John Chrysostom
32 *On the Church: Select Treatises* – St Cyprian of Carthage
33 *On the Church: Select Letters* – St Cyprian of Carthage
34 *The Book of Pastoral Rule* – St Gregory the Great
35 *Wider Than Heaven* – Homilies on the Mother of God
36 *Festal Orations* – St Gregory of Nazianzus
37 *Counsels on the Spiritual Life* – Mark the Monk
38 *On Social Justice* – St Basil the Great
39 *The Harp of Glory* – An African Akathist
40 *Divine Eros* – St Symeon the New Theologian
41 *On the Two Ways* – Foundational Texts in the Tradition
42 *On the Holy Spirit* – St Basil the Great
43 *Works on the Spirit* – Athanasius and Didymus
44 *On the Incarnation* – St Athanasius
45 *Treasure-house of Mysteries* – Poetry in the Syriac Tradition
46 *Poems on Scripture* – St Gregory of Nazianzus
47 *On Christian Doctrine and Practice* – St Basil the Great
48 *Light on the Mountain* – Homilies on the Transfiguration
49 *The Letters* – St Ignatius of Antioch
50 *On Fasting and Feasts* – St Basil the Great
51 *On Christian Ethics* – St Basil the Great
52 *Give Me a Word* – The Desert Fathers
53 *Two Hundred Chapters on Theology* – St Maximus the Confessor
54 *On the Apostolic Tradition* – Hippolytus
55 *On Pascha* – Melito of Sardis
56 *Letters to Olympia* – St John Chrysostom
57 *Lectures on the Christian Sacraments* – St Cyril of Jerusalem
58 *The Testament of the Lord*

ST VLADIMIR'S SEMINARY PRESS
1-800-204-2665 • www.svspress.com